Smitten Shepherds

Be Empowered and Encouraged
to Finish Strong!

Paul and Carolyn Wilde

Smitten Shepherds

Be Empowered and Encouraged
to Finish Strong!

Paul and Carolyn Wilde

ISBN No. 1-4961421-1-X

Dedication

Dear Pastor:

"Smitten Shepherds" is for the pastor who is still preaching and pastoring his flock. Yet he is battling discouragement from facing an exhausting attack of unceasing complaints.

This book is for the pastors who are lied about, criticized and despised. It is for the pastors who are wondering if their ministries will be effective when the gossipers have finished trying to destroy them with their venomous weapons, their tongues.

This book is for the pastors who look at their wives and their children and wonder if the hurts, weighing themselves and their families down, are worth the trouble.

This book is for the pastors who have begun to look down in discouragement or to look around at the slanderers. It is a call to look up, not only to the Author, but also to the Finisher of our faith.

We dedicate this book to you who have been called by God to speak His Word. As the care of God's people was transferred from Moses to Joshua, God knew that Joshua would need three things to finish his work.

The Lord told Moses:

1. Charge Joshua.
2. Encourage him.
3. Strengthen him.

"For he shall go over before this people, and he shall cause them to inherit the land which thou shalt see."
Deuteronomy 3:28

You have been called to lead God's people to their eternal inheritance in heaven. The battles we face along the way sometimes blind us to the inheritance in front of us. We become battle-fatigued. This is an hour when many pastors and Christian leaders who have been charged by God to tend His flock find themselves in desperate need of encouragement and strength.

Our prayer is that this book will remind you of your charge by God, encourage you as you learn you are not alone in your struggles, and strengthen you so you will be able to finish your work and fulfill the calling God has entrusted to you.

Contents

Foreword

As a district superintendent, I am always on the lookout for tools to help pastors. Paul Wilde told me about this book during a conversation with him about the two "Prophet's Chambers" his church provides for weary ministers.

After having read this manuscript, I can truly say that this book is an excellent tool for encouraging weary and embattled pastors. The approach taken in the book combines much scripture with observations and instructions that are clear and concise. Any minister (and layperson as well) will benefit greatly from the study of this book.

As a reader, I look for the content and Biblical reference. I found both throughout this book. It is my strong belief that every minister and church leader should read this book. The benefit, personally and to the kingdom, will be tremendous.

Douglas E. Fulenwider
District Superintendent
Assemblies of God Church
Louisiana District Council

Introduction

Paul and Carolyn Wilde effectively depict a major detriment to the life of the church today. Obviously, this scourge is nothing new. Faithful Christian leaders have always been subject to attack by the enemy of our souls.

From the beginning of my evangelistic work, even before I became a pastor and earned my credentials in counseling, I have sympathetically listened to the hurts and grievances of numerous pastors and missionaries. Truly, the situation is endemic.

Read this book carefully and prayerfully and do your best to encourage our church leaders so that they may finish their course with joy.

Ray Anderson—too old to retire.

Chapter 1

Shocking Comments from God's Ministers

During our nearly thirty-six years of full time service, God has richly blessed us through the ministries of some tremendous evangelists, teachers, missionaries, fellow pastors and musicians coming to our church.

Some of the pastors, evangelists and musicians you may be acquainted with are Rex Humbard, Leonard Ravenhill, Dallas Holm, Ray Comfort, Bob Harrington, Cecil Todd, Walt Mills, General Borisov, John Starnes, Quinton Mills, Ray Overholt, The Sutera Twins, Sonny Holland, Squire Parsons, Bill Britt, Billy Walker Jr., Paul Vick, Dwight Kinman, Roy Morris, Barbara Fairchild, Anthony Burger, Doug Oldham, Jimmy Wilson, Donny Sumner, Lowell Mims, Bob Martin, Simon and Philip Cameron, The McGregors, Duke and Lowell Mason, Bob and Jeannie Johnson, Dr. Shorrosh, Herb Stewart, Nazareth, Bob Cain, Brother Emmanuel, Charles Johnson & the Revivers, The Florida Boys, the Palmetto State Quartet, the Dixie Echoes, Dr. Kenny McClinton, Kyra Jackson, The Dove Brothers, H. B. London, Bob Zannini, Little Roy and the Lewis Family, The Gann Brothers, the Blackwood Brothers, Dino, Gary

McSpadden, and so many, many others.

We try to spend time with each of them, before or after the service, sometimes in a restaurant, where we talk…and where we listen.

You may be shocked by some comments made by men of God! In fact, here are a few statements God's leaders have made (paraphrased a bit, but we will let you know the actual verbatim comment later). Do you think you can put a name to each comment?

1. "I can hardly stand the people. Caring for them is too big a burden. I've gotten so depressed about it that I have asked God to kill me."

2. "I have prayed for death. I am worn out."

3. "I sometimes get so down I ask God why I was ever born."

4. "I prayed for God to let something good happen, but things didn't get better. They got worse."

5. "I can't sleep. I toss and turn all night long."

6. "I get really angry with God because He doesn't judge the sinners. I have asked Him to let me die."

7. "I don't understand why I get so down. I want to place my hope in God."

8. "It seems like the more trouble I am in, the farther away God is from me. Do you think that God hides when trouble comes?"

9. "I wonder if God has forgotten about me. Maybe He has even cast me away forever."

10. "One time, I decided to quit preaching. Another time, I decided to quit talking altogether. As you can see, that didn't last long!"

11. "I think about the people, and I want to cry all day and all night."

12. "Once I decided I would never speak in the name of the Lord again."

13. "We needed peace in our church, but it didn't come. We desperately needed a time of healing, but instead, we got more trouble."

14. "I am alone much of the time. Does God lie?"

15. "I don't know if God really hears my prayers."

16. "I have a great congregation. They come. They compliment me for the music. But their lives never change."

17. "I've begged the Lord to kill the people that treated me so badly. But He didn't."

18. "I preach faith, but when a problem arises, the people have no faith at all. I get so exhausted putting up with them."

19. "I had a church split and lost a lot of faithful people. For a while, it looked like everyone would leave. The ones who decided not to leave told me they stayed with me for only one reason—they didn't know where else to go."

20. "I expected the trials to come. What I didn't expect and I don't understand is why God would abandon me during the worst times of my life. I thought He would

be there, wrapping His arms around me and comforting me during the terrible times."

21. "I just want to go to heaven."

22. "I wish God would judge people!"

23. "I live with trouble. I stay confused. There is always a bunch talking against me. They like nothing better than to see me down."

24. "I have preached that Jesus is the only way to heaven. Is He? Or should we be looking for someone else?"

Do these comments shock you? It may shock you even more to learn who made them. First, let us look at some disturbing statistics.

Unfaithful in the Flock

Unfortunately, the church is not full of supportive people. Many do not love us or support us. Many discourage, rather than encourage. Many pray that their pastors will drop dead or leave! Many are unfaithful, not really caring whether or not churches remain open. Many stand against their pastor during the difficult times. Some spread lies and spawn hatred. Those are the ones who weigh us down and cause us to want to quit.

This book is for the fifteen hundred pastors who left the ministry last month. It is also for the three thousand pastors who will leave the ministry this month and next month.

It is for the twenty-five percent of all pastors who have been forced out of a church at some point in their ministry, either through termination or being put under intense pressure to resign.

At least fifteen percent of all churches in the United States have forced out two or more pastors. Ten percent of all United States churches have forced out three or more pastors!

It is most often just seven to ten people (three to four percent of the congregation) who drive their pastor from his fold.

The critics huddle together in a move to remove their pastor. They often find a board member to agree with them. The pastor eventually learns of the accusations. Most pastors (nearly seventy percent) meet with the discontented members in an attempt to resolve the conflict. Unfortunately, the bleating sheep have no wish to reconcile with their shepherd. The pastors are met with cold stares, hard hearts, stiff necks, and unrelenting hate-filled spirits.

Unfortunately, four out of every ten pastors who have been forced out of their churches have not yet returned to pastoral ministry.

These statistics can be read with dry eyes and a yawn. Or we can look behind the statistics and see the hurting pastors and their devastated families: pastors who entered the ministry with the hope of bringing God to a hurting generation; to make a difference in our deteriorating society—pastors who left the ministry defeated, beaten down, discouraged, hurt, and confused.

We thank every faithful, loving, loyal member of God's church who love, support, encourage and pray for their pastors.

We know you are faithful. We thank you for standing with us, through the good times and the hard times. We appreciate you.

Discouraging Times

Now let us consider the comments quoted earlier and discover who made them. Then we will look at the circumstances these men were facing that caused them to descend so low into the valley of despair.

You might be surprised to learn these comments were made from a list of heroes of the faith. You will find these quotes, prayers, moans, cries, sighs and discouraging words right in your Bible!

Those quoted are: Moses, Elijah, Job, Jonah, David, Jeremiah, Habakkuk, Ezekiel, James and John, Jesus, Paul, and John the Baptist.

Are you disturbed by some of the words coming from the mouths of these men of God, these heroes of faith?

Does it bother you that the Bible records these sighs, questions and cries for all of us—both believers and unbelievers—to read?

The Bible is a book that pulls no punches and hides nothing. In the book written by the Holy Ghost, God reveals more about His messengers than their shouts of victory. He also gives us a glimpse of their fears, despair, utter exhaustion and grief.

Would you have left your pastor in disgust if he had made even one of these statements?

Would you have canceled plans to hear your favorite evangelist if you were told he made one of these comments?

Would you have thrown away your favorite singer's recordings if you heard he had dared to question God and His Word in his time of discouragement?

Will you throw out the heroes of your Bible? Will you rip all mention of Moses, Elijah, Job, Jonah, David, Jeremiah, Habakkuk, Ezekiel, James, John, Paul, John the Baptist and Jesus from the pages of God's Word?

What caused our Bible heroes to make these statements and ask these questions?

This book will examine why they were exhausted and discouraged.

Chapter 2

Impossible Expectations

We live in a day of unreal expectations.

It is hard for us to believe that Jesus was ever physically tired. We can believe that He walked on water, but it shocks us to know that He grew tired of His faithless people.

God never commands His spokesmen to stay perpetually happy,

> to never get tired,
> to never be weighed down with a burden,
> to never be confused,
> to never be disappointed,
> to never be discouraged.

But that is what the church expects of its leaders. This "feel good, be happy" generation expects pastors to go through their days singing, go to bed smiling and wake up grinning—whatever the circumstances.

Jesus tells us to join Him in ministry, and gives this promise with His call: "For **my yoke** is easy, and **my burden** is light." *Matthew 11:30*

His yoke is easy. The problem is that **man's yoke** is

anything but easy. It is hard. As a result of the unreasonable yoke that has been placed upon pastors, they are simply walking away from their calling. The current statistic is that 1,500 pastors are leaving the ministry every single month. That adds up to eighteen thousand weary, discouraged pastors walking away from their churches every single year. They cannot live up to the expectations of their congregations or even to their own expectations. Their families can never be what their critics want them to be. They quit, because they can't stand the constant, unceasing pressure.

Denying the Truth

Our world is in trouble. Our nation is in trouble. Our neighborhoods are in trouble. Our marriages are in trouble. Our children are in trouble. Our churches are in trouble. And many of our preachers are in trouble.

Is it a time to go around, spouting cheerful clichés and ignoring the grief around us? American churchgoers do not want facts—they want fantasy.

"For the time will come when they **will not endure** sound doctrine; but after their own lusts shall they heap to themselves teachers, having itching ears; and they shall turn away their ears from the truth, and **shall be turned unto fables**." *II Timothy 4:3-4*

Fables are **falsehoods; folk tales; fabrications; or lies.**

"Can't you soften your message," Martin Luther was asked after one of his thundering sermons.

"Your message offends people."

Luther's answer came with a scoff, as he held up his Bible. "What good does the edge of the sword do if it does not cut?"

God instructed the prophet Isaiah to write a book and give His people this message: "Now go, write it before them in a table, and note it in a book, that it may be for the time to come for ever and ever: that this is a rebellious people, lying children, children that will not hear the law of the LORD: which say to the seers, See not; and to the prophets, Prophesy not unto us right things, **speak unto us smooth things**, prophesy deceits." *Isaiah 30:8-10*

God's people prefer to hear comforting lies rather than the revealing truth. This is true of our nation and it is true of our churches.

We don't want to hear terror alerts. If Homeland Security issues an alert today, and the terrorists do not destroy someone or something within a week, we are disgusted with Homeland Security for upsetting us.

We don't want our leaders to tell us that our wars may be prolonged.

If we are involved in a war, we expect to: Get in. Get out. And get home!

It is okay with us if the Weather Bureau issues a hurricane, tornado or flood warning. We know the storm will come quickly and we can prepare. But if there is a weather report from God, such as Noah received, we don't want to be bothered. Thankfully, Noah was not like the church of our day. He and his family faithfully prepared for the flood for over 100 years.

Jesus warned, "And as it was in the days of Noah, so shall it be also in the days of the Son of man. They did eat, they drank, they married wives, they were given in marriage, until the day that Noah entered into the ark, and the flood came, and destroyed them all." *Luke 17:26-27*

Congregations today demand a feel-good, be happy, joke-telling pastor. Prophets who tell the truth are labeled "doomsday preachers." Evangelists who preach judgments are called "hellfire and damnation preachers." Pastors who add rebuking and reproving to their ministry of shepherding their flocks are either voted out of the church or the "feel good bunch" leaves the church in disgust.

And the church continues its blood-letting—its life drained as its leaders leave.

Many who leave their calling view themselves as total failures. They forget that wanting to quit comes with the calling! Our Bible heroes of the faith wanted to walk away too! But there was one big difference between them and the 18,000 pastors who actually walk away from God's call on their lives every year.

Our heroes of the faith kept the faith and kept going!

Chapter 3

Endurance

MOSES

Moses sighed to God: "I can hardly stand the people. Caring for them is too big a burden. I've gotten so low about it, that I want You to just kill me." *(See Numbers 11:14-15.)*

Yes, the burden of the people became too much—***but Moses kept carrying it.***

He picked up the burden of leading God's rebellious people, placed it on his back, and ended his earthly ministry with a powerful sermon to prepare the new generation to enter the promised land.

"Be strong and of a good courage," he instructed young Joshua.

He knew that strength and courage is a must for every leader in God's army.

Our last picture of Moses is not in the Old Testament, but in the New. We see him standing with Jesus on the mountain where Jesus was transfigured. (He couldn't make it to the Promised Land through the law of the Old Testament, but he made it in through Jesus!)

Moses kept going—and he reached the Promised Land!

ELIJAH

We think of mighty Elijah as the great prayer warrior. The New Testament reminds us of his prayer that shut the heavens, and his prayer three and a half years later that opened the heavens and ended the drought.

But do we also remember this prayer by Elijah?

"It is enough; now, O LORD, take away my life." *(See I Kings 19:4.)*

God is a prayer answering God. Elijah proved it to us!

He wanted to die, so he prayed that God would kill him.

And he waited for God to answer. And he waited....

He decided a good place to die would be underneath a juniper tree.

Instead of killing him, God sent an angel to prepare a meal for him. The angel not only had to cook and deliver the food, but also had to wake him up and force him to eat.

Elijah ate. One last meal. Then he wearily laid back down, waiting anxiously for the answer to his prayer.

That was one prayer that God never did answer.

Elijah not only didn't die then, he **never** died!

Elijah eventually got up from his bed, began anew his

ministry of prophecy, and was chauffeured into heaven in a chariot of fire! Christ's disciples saw him on the mountain, conversing with Jesus and Moses.

Elijah could have refused to get back up when things were bleak and his prayer wasn't answered.

But Elijah kept going.

JOB

Job. He's the one who makes all our problems seem small.

Job made it through a time of utter darkness in his life. We remember his cries of victory: "Naked came I out of my mother's womb, and naked shall I return thither: the LORD gave, and the LORD hath taken away; blessed be the name of the LORD. What? Shall we receive good at the hand of God, and shall we not receive evil?" *Job 1:21*

But do we recall his words when despair gripped him, and he cried out to God in the night hours: "Why died I not from the womb? Why did I not give up the ghost when I came out of the belly? When I looked for good, then evil came unto me: and when I waited for light, there came darkness!"

When he went to bed, he couldn't sleep. He moaned, "I am full of tossings to and fro unto the dawning of the day."

God called His servant perfect.

His friends called him a no-good, wicked sinner.

Job spent his nights longing for daylight. But when the sun rose, he begged for night. *(See Job 3:11; 30:26; 7:4.)*

Job made it through his time of loss, unending pain and turmoil to live an additional 140 years, birth ten more children, and be honored at a party surrounded by friends who showered him with gifts. He lived to enjoy a twofold increase of blessings from God! Job even made it into the pages of the New Testament. James reminds us of him and his victory over pain: "Behold, we count them happy which endure. Ye have heard of the patience of Job, and have seen the end of the Lord; that the Lord is very pitiful, and of tender mercy." *James 5:11*

Job could have quit. He chose to keep going!

Jonah

Even rebellious Jonah finished his task as the Lord's spokesman!

He was furious that God didn't destroy the city of Nineveh. He had tried to get out of this job and ended up in a fish's stomach. He described his adventure as being in the belly of hell, with weeds wrapped around his head. He tells us that his soul fainted.

Finally the fish vomited him out of its stomach. As Jonah lay on the beach in the vomit of the whale, he decided he'd better obey the Lord.

He spoke, revival came, and the judgment of God was avoided.

Jonah was furious. He begged to die. He didn't want revival—he wanted judgment! He had not wanted to go to Nineveh because he was worried they would repent and be salvaged. He wanted God to kill these wretched enemies of Israel. Why should he go warn them of their impending doom? He finally went, but he didn't preach repentance and he offered no altar call.

There was no rejoicing on Jonah's part when the king ordered fasting, prayer and repentance. He left the revival, built himself a little booth outside the city, and sat down to watch, waiting and still hoping that God would kill the 120,000 inhabitants of Nineveh. God, in His great mercy, spared them.

But even Jonah kept going. He was referred to in II Kings 14:25 as God's messenger: "...according to the word of the LORD God of Israel, which he spake by the hand of ***his servant Jonah***, the son of Amittai, the prophet..."

DAVID

Many times David asked his soul why it was so cast down. He wondered why he was downhearted and depressed. Why wasn't he hoping in God?

It was King David who asked the Lord why He was so far away and even dared to pray: "Why do you hide when I'm in trouble? Why have you forgotten me?"

Then, as if being forgotten by God was not bad enough, David asked God why He had cast him off!

Can you envision David, surrounded by enemies and trouble, wondering in despair and discouragement if God had cast him away and had no more use for him?

"Awake, why sleepest thou, O Lord?" David cried out to God!

We often read in the Scriptures that God tells **us** to wake up. But here is David, begging God to wake up and asking why He is sleeping when He is so desperately needed!

We picture David faithfully singing praises and strumming his harp through his rough times. The Bible gives us another glimpse of David. We hear him asking God why He is taking a nap! Why was David so desperate for immediate help that he was moved to question God?

David was hated—and he didn't like it.

He said, "All that hate me whisper together against me: against me do they devise my hurt."

Then David was betrayed by a trusted friend—and he didn't like that either.

"Mine own familiar friend, in whom I trusted, which did eat of my bread, hath lifted up his heel against me. For it was not an enemy that reproached me; then I could have borne it: neither was it he that hated me that did magnify himself against me; then I would have hid myself from him: but it was thou, a man mine equal, my guide, and mine acquaintance. We took sweet counsel together, and walked unto the house of God in company." *Psalm 55:12-15*

David was heartsick.

"My heart is sore pained within me."

David was afraid. (David? Who marched up to Goliath with a slingshot and five stones?) Yes, this same David. Listen to his admission: "Fearfulness and trembling are come upon me, and horror hath overwhelmed me."

David, our hero of faith, could think of only one solution. "Oh that I had wings like a dove! For then would I fly away, and be at rest." And where would David fly away to if he had wings? He had a place in mind.

"Then would I wander far off, and remain in the wilderness. I would hasten my escape from the windy storm and tempest."

He begged God to destroy those who hated him.

"Destroy, O Lord, and divide their tongues...let death seize upon them, and let them go down quick into hell."

When judgment didn't fall, we see David—the Psalmist of praise and worship—asking God why He was hiding.

"Why hidest thou thy face from me?"

We can almost hear the sounds of beautiful music coming from the songbook of our Bibles, penned and sung by David, the beloved Psalmist. But do we also see him with his face buried in his hands, his song silenced?

"I was dumb with silence," he wrote. "I held my peace, even from good; and my sorrow was stirred."

But David didn't quit. He didn't quit singing. He didn't quit praising God. Why? Listen....

"My heart was hot within me, while I was musing the fire burned: then spake I with my tongue." *(See Psalm 42:5-6; 43:5; 42:11; 10:1; 42:9; 43:2; 44:23; 88:14; 39:2-3.)*

There was a divine call of God upon David. There was a message in David's heart, and it burned like fire. David tried to, but could not quit speaking, singing, and praising.

King David ended his reign victoriously. He reminded us in his old age: "I have been young, and now am old; yet have I not seen the righteous forsaken, nor his seed begging bread." *Psalm 37:25*

David kept going.

JEREMIAH

Jeremiah's fifty-two chapters are included in the Bible. We think of him as a faithful and victorious prophet of God.

Jeremiah wouldn't have been a sought after pastor in today's culture. He is often referred to as the "weeping prophet."

Hear his cry: "Oh that my head were waters, and mine eyes a fountain of tears, that I might weep day and night...."

Buried within the pages of his prophecies and visions are these words: "...the word of the LORD was made a reproach unto me, and a derision, daily."

Every single day, Jeremiah spent his life warning God's people of coming judgments. They rewarded him with sneers, mockery and ridicule.

He finally had enough of prophesying to the sneering crowd.

No one was listening to him.

He had no converts—not even one.

So he decided to quit.

"Then I said I will not make mention of him, nor speak any more in his name."

But like David, Jeremiah had an anointing fire burning within his heart. He could not quit, in spite of the cost.

"But his word was in mine heart as a burning fire shut up in my bones, and I was weary with forbearing, and I could not stay."

He continued to speak God's Word. He continued to put up with the insults and humiliating jeers.

But it did not get easier for him. Years went by. The promised judgments did not fall. Was God's Word true? Jeremiah wondered where the great Physician and Comforter had gone. Where was God?

He looked up to the heavens and asked: "Is there no balm in Gilead; is there no physician there?"

Mockers continued mocking and Jeremiah was alone, even in a crowd.

"I sat not in the assembly of the mockers, nor rejoiced; I sat alone because of thy hand: for thou hast filled me with indignation. Why is my pain perpetual, and my wound incurable, which refuseth to be healed? Wilt thou be altogether unto me as a liar, and as waters that fail?" *(See Jeremiah 9:1, 8-9; 20:8-9; 8:22; 14:19; 15:16-18.)*

No, God was not a liar. One by one, God's Words were fulfilled.

Did Jeremiah then become a hero among the people?

No. He was thrown into a pit and sank in the mud. He had no water to drink and no food to eat. He was nearly dead when thirty men arrived with ropes to rescue him. They ordered Jeremiah to place the rags and ropes under his armpits. Then they began the torturous job of dragging him out of the mire.

Jeremiah was never regarded as a spokesman for God by the people of his day, but the New Testament reminds us of his message.

And is not the opinion of God more valuable than the opinion of men?

Jeremiah kept going.

HABAKKUK

Then there was the prophet, Habakkuk. Let's listen in on one of his prayers.

"O LORD, how long shall I cry, and thou wilt not hear! Even cry out unto thee of violence, and thou wilt not save! Why dost thou show me iniquity, and cause me to behold grievance? For spoiling and violence are before me: and there are that raise up strife and contention."

There are that raise up strife and contention....

Strife is ***discord; conflict; or unrest***.

Contention is ***argument; battle; rivalry; opposition; controversy; or resistance***.

Wherever we see a true man of God speaking the true message of God, strife and contention are always present.

Habakkuk kept speaking God's Word, in spite of the constant strife and unending contention. He ended his biography with this shout of determination and triumph:

"Although the fig tree shall not blossom, neither shall fruit be in the vines; the labour of the olive shall fail, and the fields shall yield no meat; the flock shall be cut off from the fold, and there shall be no herd in the stalls: Yet I will rejoice in the LORD, I will joy in the God of my salvation. The LORD God is my strength, and he will make my feet like hinds' feet, and he will make me to walk upon mine high places." *(See Habakkuk 1:2-3 and 3:17-19.)*

Habakkuk kept going.

EZEKIEL

Ezekiel had to face the truth about his congregation. They were wonderful—to his face. They talked about how much they loved him and how much they loved God. They filled his church. They loved his singing and marveled at his ability to play well on his instrument. They complimented his sermons, recognizing them as the true Word of God. They invited everyone they met to come hear him preach.

But God and Ezekiel knew the truth about these people—and it was discouraging. God told Ezekiel: "Also, thou son of man, the children of thy people still are talking against thee by the walls and in the doors of the houses, and speak one to another, every one to his brother, saying,

Come, I pray you, and hear what is the word that cometh forth from the LORD. And they come unto thee as the people cometh, and they sit before thee as my people, and **they hear** thy words, but **they will not do** them: for with their **mouth** they show much love, but their **heart** goeth after their covetousness. And, lo, thou art unto them as a very lovely song of one that hath a pleasant voice, and can play well on an instrument: for they **hear** thy words, but they **do them not**." *Ezekiel 33:30-32*

Week after week, Ezekiel's congregation heard what he had to say, but their lives never changed. They loved to **hear**, but refused to **do**, the Word of the Lord.

There are few things that are as discouraging for a pastor.

But Ezekiel kept going.

JOHN THE BAPTIST

John was called by God from his womb to announce the coming of the Messiah to earth. He faithfully fulfilled his call. He stirred his hearers by denouncing their sinful lives. Some were stirred to repentance. Others were stirred to hatred.

And John? He ended up in a dungeon. It was there, and it was then, that the doubts plagued him. If his job was so vital that it was prophesied in the Old Testament, why was his body tossed like a filthy rag into this rat-infested hole?

He was finally able to send a messenger to Jesus with his question.

"Art thou he that should come, or do we look for another?" *Matthew 11:2-3*

This same John, who introduced Jesus to his listeners with this announcement: "Behold the Lamb of God, which taketh away the sin of the world," was now filled with doubts.

Jesus did not rebuke John for his question. Instead, He sent an encouraging message back to the discouraged prophet.

"Go and show John again those things which ye do hear and see: The blind receive their sight, and the lame walk, the lepers are cleansed, and the deaf hear, the dead are raised up, and the poor have the gospel preached to them. And ***blessed is he, whosoever shall not be offended in me.***"

While the messengers left to take John the message, Jesus spoke to the people about John. He praised the prophet who was banished to the lonely dungeon. He praised the prophet who was given a Word from heaven, but was left with no congregation to hear it.

"And as they departed, Jesus began to say unto the multitudes concerning John, What went ye out into the wilderness to see? A reed shaken with the wind? But what went ye out for to see? A man clothed in soft raiment? Behold, they that wear soft clothing are in kings' houses. But what went ye out for to see? A prophet? Yea, I say unto you, and more than a prophet. For this is he, of whom it is written, Behold, I send ***my messenger*** before thy face, which shall prepare thy way before thee."

"Verily I say unto you, among them that are born of women there hath not risen a greater than John the Baptist: notwithstanding he that is least in the kingdom of heaven is greater than he. And from the days of John the Baptist until now the kingdom of heaven suffereth violence, and the violent take it by force."

"For all the prophets and the law prophesied until John. And if ye will receive it, this is Elias, which was for to come. He that hath ears to hear, let him hear. For John came neither eating nor drinking, and they say, He hath a devil." *Matthew 11:4-15, 18*

While the people condemned, Jesus praised His servant.

"Don't be offended, John. God has everything under control. You will be blessed in the end if you are not offended because of Me...."

How many pastors have quit ministering in the name of Jesus because they were offended when they were lied about, scoffed and mocked?

Jesus called the filthy man in the filthy dungeon **His** messenger. He called him great.

Only those <u>with spiritual ears</u> would understand that he was a messenger sent from the throne of God.

All others look for a messenger of God who meets their standards. He should be pliable—a "reed shaken with the wind." He should be moldable, so he can be shaped into their image. He should wear fine, soft clothing. He should not come dressed in camel's hair and a leather girdle.

Let's listen in on the comments....

"We told him to soften his message. But he wouldn't."

"He could have kept the crowds if he hadn't called us a generation of vipers. Who does he think he is?"

"Why does he keep insisting on repentance and restitution?"

"If he had really been sent by God, he wouldn't have ended up in a dungeon."

"He wouldn't have landed in the dungeon in the first place if he had just kept quiet about Herod sleeping with his sister-in-law."

An angel announced that John was coming with these words before his birth: ***He shall be great <u>in the sight of the Lord</u>....*** *Luke 1:15*

Great in the sight of the Lord....

Who cares if the people call a man of God a devil, if, in God's sight, he is great?

Plots were hatched and John was executed.

God has many great messengers buried in the holes of this earth.

John remained in his dungeon until his death.

John kept going, through the dungeon, through death, and received a hero's welcome in heaven.

"He shall be great in the sight of the Lord...."

JAMES AND JOHN

James and John gave up their business and left their homes to follow Jesus. They probably expected great things as they joined themselves to the Messiah, the water-walker, the dead-raiser, the multitude-feeder. They may have even expected to be treated with respect among the people.

They weren't. One village refused to even sell them food for their journey. They were fed up with being treated badly. They begged Jesus to call down fire from heaven. They would have liked to see the village burned up. (*See Luke 9:54-56.*)

Jesus rebuked them.

The village never did sell them groceries.

Fire did not fall from heaven.

But James and John kept going, not taking lives, but giving theirs freely, even to martyrdom.

JESUS

Jesus got tired of teaching His disciples. He turned to them one day with these scathing words: "O faithless and perverse generation, how long shall I be with you? How long shall I suffer you?" *Matthew 17:17*

His disciples must have been shocked to be called faithless and perverted!

Then they heard, "How long shall I suffer—***endure; tolerate; stomach***—you?"

Here is Isaiah's description of our Lord:

"He is despised and rejected of men; a man of sorrows, and acquainted with grief: and we hid as it were our faces from him; he was despised, and we esteemed him not." *Isaiah 53:3*

What church would accept Him as its pastor? Yet this is the Founder and Head of the Church; our Savior; our Lord; our King; our Beloved; our Groom; our God.

We are told that Jesus was weary, sorrowful, misunderstood, called the devil, and suspected of insanity by members of His own family.

He watched His followers walk away from Him and His congregation split.

He asked His twelve disciples (one of them a devil) if they were leaving too, but they replied that there was no one else to go to, so they would stay. *(See John 6:66-71.)*

The crowds wanted to kill Him throughout His ministry, simply because He told them the truth.

"But now ye seek to kill me, a man that hath told you the truth, which I have heard of God." *John 8:40*

He endured the cross and despised its shame. Psalm 22 gives us a glimpse of the suffering Jesus endured: "I am poured out like water, and all my bones are out of joint: my heart is like wax; it is melted in the midst of my bowels. My strength is dried up like a potsherd; and my tongue cleaveth to my jaws; and thou hast brought me into the dust of death...the assembly of the wicked have enclosed me: they pierced my hands and my feet. I may tell **(identify)** all my bones: they look and stare upon me. They part my garments among them, and cast lots upon my vesture...***be not thou far from me, O LORD: O my strength, haste thee to help me.***"

"Be not far from me...."

Yet Jesus did not feel His Father's presence that dark day. He cried from His cross: "My God, my God, why hast **thou** forsaken me?"

Men hated him so intensely that they posted guards at His tomb, lest He get up and walk among the living once again. He did.

Jesus came out of His tomb and kept going.

PAUL

Paul was the one who longed to die and go to heaven. Listen to his admission: "For I am in a strait betwixt two, having a desire to depart, and to be with Christ; which is far better."

Paul was the one who wanted the church's persecutors cut off (killed). "I would they were even cut off which trouble you." Paul was the one who said he was

"...troubled on every side, yet not distressed;

perplexed ***(flustered)***, but not in despair;

persecuted, but not forsaken;

cast down, but not destroyed."

It was Paul who called his congregation in Galatia a foolish, bewitched church. It was Paul who said his congregation would have plucked out their eyes and given them to him when they first heard him. But the "honeymoon" was soon over as Paul spoke the truth. Their love turned to hatred. His friends turned into enemies.

"If it had been possible, ye would have plucked out your own eyes, and have given them to me. Am I therefore become your enemy, because I tell you the truth?" *Galatians 4:15-16*

Paul kept going. He ended his earthly journey with this final shout of victory: "I have fought a good fight! I have finished my course: I have kept the faith!" *(See Philippians 1:23; Galatians 5:12; II Corinthians 4:8-12; Galatians 3:1.)*

Paul kept going.

Chapter 4

18,000 Quit

Fifteen hundred pastors every month choose not to keep going. They quit. Preachers lose their joy and simply walk away from God's call on their lives saying, "I don't have to put up with this! I quit!"

A common joke among preachers is that they resign every Monday. The problem is that it isn't a joke. Many do resign.

Many in today's church do not want to hear the Word of God. Congregations want to come out of church on Sundays happy, but the Bible says: "For godly sorrow worketh repentance." *II Corinthians 7:10*

Many in our congregations want nothing that would cause them sorrow. They do not want to hear warnings, rebukes, or reproofs. They never want to see disappointment or grief in their leaders.

God never paints a picture of an easy life of endless glee for His people. "In the world ye shall have tribulation: but be of good cheer; I have overcome the world." *John 16:33*

We like the "be of good cheer" part. We skip over the tribulation part. Tribulation is ***distress; trial; difficulty;***

loss; vexation; or suffering.

Any man of God who speaks the whole Word of God is not going to be accepted by the modern day church. As he speaks truth, he will be hated. Being hated is not fun.

"Many are the afflictions ***(hardships; difficulties; agonies)*** of the righteous: but the LORD delivereth him out of them all." *Psalm 34:19*

God Himself, as He looks at His creation and the suffering that rebellion has brought to their lives, cries from His heart of grief: "O that there were such an heart in them, that they would fear me, and keep all my commandments always, that it might be well with them, and with their children for ever!" *Deuteronomy 5:29*

God described the sin of Sodom and Gomorrah as very grievous. In other words, there was grief in the very heart of God.

The Scriptures describe the Christian life as warfare.

When is war fun? When soldiers enlist and go to war, it is expected that they will face an enemy. It is possible that they will be injured and even killed.

When a fireman answers a summons, he knows he may face danger and may even be called upon to give his life to save someone.

Every policeman knows he will be hated by lawbreakers and may be killed, simply because he represents the law of the land.

Every leader who governs in any capacity knows his motives and his life and the lives of his family members will be examined and probed, open to public debate and discussion, and subjected to constant criticism.

Add to these professions a relentless enemy that wants nothing more than to stop the mouths of God's spokesmen. Satan does not want his plans for the destruction of the human race revealed. His hatred of God and his expulsion from heaven has filled him with rage.

Satan's hatred of God causes him to attack what God loves. He attacked God's only beloved Son. He now attacks every soul winner, every pastor, every singer, every missionary, every evangelist and every prophet who dares to herald heaven's good news: "Jesus saves!"

People who despise messengers of God do not even realize where their boiling hatred has originated. Satan literally fills people with an illogical, intense hatred.

God has never painted a life of ease for His representatives. Any man who has been called by God to speak in His name and minister His love should know that he will have to deal with people and their unreasonable expectations. He should realize he has a powerful enemy and will have to face the wrath of the devil. Jesus warned that His followers will face hatred and betrayal by friends and family members. Being hated is not enjoyable. Yet it comes with the calling.

We didn't realize that we would also face disappointment in ourselves. Somehow we expected to keep laughing our way through all the hurt and grief that the ministry brings. When we find ourselves discouraged and down and sometimes hopeless and helpless, the accuser of the brethren moves in on us.

His questions bombard us and rob us of peace.

"What is wrong with **you?**"

"Do you really think God called **you?**"

"If **you** were called by God, don't you think you would be more successful than you are? Don't you think you would have a bigger congregation? Don't you think that your people would love you?"

We must learn to answer, "No. My King called me into the ministry with this warning: ***Ye shall be hated of all nations for my name's sake.***" *Matthew 24:9*

We tire because of the endless demands of our time. We find our bodies are not transformed into a superhuman state when we enter the ministry. We still get weary. We still get nervous. We still get worried. We still need sleep. We still need a time of rest. Our work never gets done.

We don't even have to look outside our own church walls to find sinners, hurting people, sick people, dying people, hungry people, angry people, jobless people, unloved spouses, and unloved children.

We find the lonely, confused, elderly, disabled, fearful, and backslidden people.

If we dare, we do look outside our church walls and find unsaved people, dying people—and the list goes on, and on, and on, and on.

If we risk looking far (or close) enough, we will find our nation in trouble. As pastors, surely we should be doing something about abortion, crumbling morals, problems in our schools, and the 35,000 children worldwide starving to death every single day.

If we risk looking at the globe, we find we are not doing enough to strengthen and support discouraged missionaries. And what of the fields that are white unto harvest? Should we go on a mission trip rather than on a vacation?

We flee to our Bibles for comfort and read our instructions for the day.

> Comfort the feeble minded.
> Care for the widows.
> Visit the sick.
> Minister to the prisoners.
> Feed the hungry.
> Clothe the needy.
> Preach the Word.
> Reprove and rebuke the disobedient.
> Go into all the world and preach the gospel to every
>   creature.
> Study.
> Pray without ceasing.
> Meditate on the Scriptures day and night.

We look in our homes for comfort and we hear more of God's instructions.

Provide for your family.

Love your wife.

Teach your children.

We wonder if we are teaching or neglecting our family, as we care for the needs of the church family. Are we spending enough time teaching our children?

We open our Bible and see this command: "...thou shalt teach (these words) diligently unto thy children, and shalt talk of them when thou sittest in thine house, and when thou walkest by the way, and when thou liest down, and when thou risest up." *Deuteronomy 6:6-7*

A thousand lifetimes of work could not meet all the needs. We could work twenty-four hours a day for the rest of our lives and never fulfill the expectations of church members, fellow citizens, family members, and even ourselves.

How can we please God when we can't possibly do all that He has told us to do? We begin to feel guilty when we rest. Unfortunately, the accuser of the brethren never seems to rest.

It is enough that others grumble against us and the devil harasses us. Then we add our own accusations and get down on ourselves. It is often our own failed expectations that bring the final crushing blow.

We deal with the disgruntled on Sundays and then with our own selves on Mondays.

There is a vast difference between conviction and condemnation.

God gives conviction—and ***always accompanies it with a solution.***

Conviction in our hearts brings repentance.

God not only convicts us, He leads us to confession and repentance.

If there is someone we need to love, forgive or apologize to, He tells us.

If there is something we are neglecting that we need to make a priority in our lives, He tells us.

If the world has crept in and is robbing us of a closer walk with Him, He tells us.

If we need to come apart and rest awhile, He tells us.

If sin is hindering our close fellowship with Him, He instructs us to confess it and forsake it.

But condemnation...it is guilt without a solution. It comes from the enemy of our souls to wear us down when we are already worn out. Discouragement settles into our spirits.

Our pace slows to a crawl....

Chapter 5

God's Servant

Constant criticism wears us down and steals our joy. It seems our congregations will not and cannot ever be satisfied with anything we do. There is always a long list of things we have left undone. We know it and they know it.

Though they have never pastored; preached a sermon; conducted a funeral; dealt with the tensions of a wedding; put a church back together after a vicious split; stood against the constant bombardment of the devil who is determined to "smite the shepherd so the sheep will be scattered;" agonized over a decision that is going to be costly and will involve souls; been on call 365 days a year, 24 hours a day; and never faced the unceasing criticisms from the congregation—they have **all** the answers, in **every** situation of exactly what we should do; what we should wear; where we should live; what car we should drive; what music we should sing; what prayers we should pray; what sermons we should preach; what we should do with our leisure time; how many hours (if any) we should sleep; where we should go on vacation (it makes little difference, as we are too tired to enjoy it); how much we should weigh; how our children should behave; and whose hand we should shake first.

And woe be unto us if we ever reprove and rebuke when things get nasty.

The average church member wants

a leader who does not lead;

a pastor who is never discouraged;

a human who has no need of rest or

sleep.

Can we be what the people want us to be? **Never.**

Can we be what **we** want us to be? **Never.**

Can we be what the Lord wants us to be? Unbelievably— yes!

We can simply listen to His voice—

not the complaining voices of men—

not the accusing voice of Satan—

not even our own accusing voice—

but day by day,

moment by moment,

do what God

tells us to do.

Jesus said, "My sheep hear my voice, and I know them, and _**they follow me**_."

We must realize we cannot do everything by ourselves. We will never please our critics. Yes, a shepherd is yoked to his flock, and daily responsibilities come with that yoke.

However, a pastor will never fulfill the people's expectations of him.

A pastor's wife will be unable to fulfill the expectations of the people. What satisfies some of the members will infuriate others.

A pastor's children will never be able to be the model children that the congregation wants them to be. Parents are instructed to train their children, because they arrive needing training. **All children arrive this way.** Unfortunately, this includes pastor's children.

It is impossible to please the people. God instructs His people not to be "...menpleasers; but as the servants of Christ, doing **the will of God** from the heart; with good will doing service, **as to the Lord, and not to men."** *Ephesians 6:6-7*

Our one priority is to listen to the still small voice of our Shepherd and follow Him. **His** yoke is the **only** yoke that is easy.

If you have pleased Him, it is enough.

He is our Master. We are His servants. When we become His servants, we become servants and ministers, not **of** mankind, but **to** mankind.

The question is asked of the congregation in Romans 14:4: "Who art thou that judgest another man's servant? To his own master he standeth or falleth...."

"So we, being **many, are one** body in Christ."

Jesus did not attempt to please the people. In fact, He displeased them so much that they crucified Him.

Peter wrote, "...ye should follow his steps." *I Peter 2:21*

How did our Lord walk?

He tells us: "...I do always **_those things that please him._**"

This is the only way we will survive the ministry.

God's Word commands us to do a multitude of things, including going into all the world and preaching the gospel to every creature. God has shown us the only way to accomplish our tasks. He calls on the body of Christ to do His work.

"...ye are the body of Christ, and members in particular."

God expects His work to get done on this earth. He expects the sick, the imprisoned, the hungry, the sinners, the heartbroken, the feeble-minded, the widows, the aged, and the backslidden to be ministered to. But He expects His entire body to do the work, not one man, who has been hired by lazy and complacent people, to do it all. Yes, every church has a group of faithful, willing workers. But the harvest is great and the laborers too few, in the church as a whole and in each church in particular.

God's Word compares His body to our bodies.

Our eyes do not do everything. They are required only to see.

Our ears do not do everything. They were created only to hear.

Our toes do not do everything. They were made to help us keep our balance while walking.

Even our mouth does not do everything!

If a pastor has been hired by a congregation made up of shiftless members, he will soon fall far short of their expectations. They know there is work to do, but they expect the pastor to do everything in their church, neighborhood, and city. They have hired him to do their praying, studying, teaching, witnessing and visiting.

Do you remember what drove our Lord to fashion a whip and drive people from the temple? The people who were supposed to bring a sacrifice were **buying** a sacrifice! What angered Jesus then is sure to anger Him today. People buy a pastor to be their sacrifice, while they remain idle and the fields remain unharvested. It is not God's plan!

The pastor will wear himself out as he attempts to prepare the field, purchase the seed, sow the seed, pray for the rain, pray for the sunshine, pray away the storms, harvest the crops, prepare the food for consumption and then distribute the food to the hungry.

Many people, again in our day, want to go to the temple and give money to purchase their sacrifice. They offer their purchased pastor to the Lord. They do nothing themselves in the field of harvest. It is not God's way! It will doom their pastor to failure. The pastor will wear out. All the work cannot possibly get done. One man cannot do it. A few men cannot do it. It takes the entire body, each functioning as God ordains, to fulfill the work of God in a church and in a city.

When all the needs are not met and jobs remain undone, complainers will begin to complain and critics will begin to criticize. Soon there is an undercurrent of tension in the church. Telephones begin to ring.

"Don't you think our church would do better with a new pastor? This one seems pretty worn out."

Countless pastors have been fired by their parishioners at least once. The chance of a pastor being fired is now higher than the chance of a football coach being fired.

The disheartened pastor will begin anew with more unreasonable demands and more impossible expectations—

in another church;

with another congregation.

Chapter 6

Down in the Valley

Unfulfilled hopes begin to weigh on a pastor until he sags under a heavy burden of discouragement. Many pastors descend into the valley of despair. The descent into the valley is not a sudden thud. One day he wakes up and finds he is no longer living on the mountain. Somehow he has fallen to the depths of the valley and has no strength to begin the climb out.

The valleys come to everyone's life.

> Loved ones die.
> Friendships fail.
> Hopes fade.
> God's promises tarry.

While others mourn, the pastor comforts. When a church disturbance comes, the pastor tries to ignore the hurt in his own heart while mending his wounded sheep.

The view in the valley isn't very good. We are surrounded by mountains that we are too weary to climb. The sun isn't shining as brightly. Then comes the nagging question that robs us of joy and sleep:

"What are we doing down here anyway? We're supposed to be happy!"

Condemnation creeps into our thoughts.

How can we effectively pastor while sitting in a valley—discouraged—staring at mountains all around us and dreading the climb out?

What is wrong with us?

Who are we to pastor others?

If anyone still wonders if pastors face temptation, the answer is YES! The biggest temptation of every pastor is to give up and quit!

Did you know that Martin Luther was tempted to quit in despair? He taught the Scriptures to his congregation at a rapid pace, determined to pack them full of the Word of God. This was his weekly teaching schedule:

Sunday at 5:00 a.m.	**Pauline Epistles**
Sunday at 9:00 a.m.	**The Gospels**
Sunday Afternoon	**The Catechism**
Monday	**The Catechism**
Tuesday	**The Catechism**
Wednesday	**The Gospel of Matthew**
Thursday	**The Epistles**
Friday	**The Epistles**
Saturday	**The Gospel of John**

(Hunger for God's Word is sadly lacking in today's church. Who would gather to hear Luther's teachings in our day? Three services a week are an overload for most congregations.)

Luther not only taught the Bible and preached his sermons, he sang, strummed his lute and played his flute. He penned over 60,000 pages of Bible teachings. He turned his entire congregation into his choir. He married Katherina, a feisty, redheaded, twenty-six year old ex-nun when he was forty-two. (He made the comment to a friend, "If I should ever marry again, I would hew myself an obedient wife out of stone.")

Martin and Katie had six noisy children. They adopted four more noisy children. Martin brought home needy students, the homeless, the sick and the dying. Katie took care of the orchard, fish pond, barnyard, harvested the fruit, caught the fish and slaughtered the pigs. She fed twenty-five or thirty people around her table daily. Martin gave away what money he had and never concerned himself with the problem of feeding his household. He left that to God and Katie.

We read about Martin and Katie's lives and feel worthless. How did they keep such a pace? Did Martin ever get discouraged?

He did. He retreated to his valley (in his case, his study) more than once, bowed down with depression. He would refuse to come out, locking himself in for three days at a time. Katie would put up with it for a while, but when she'd had enough of his gloom, she simply removed the door from the hinges.

Once when Katie noticed a deep discouragement settling over her husband, she tried as she usually did to cheer him, but nothing she did worked. Martin was unwilling to begin his climb out of the valley.

He was bombarded with betrayals and misunderstandings of friends. Vicious rumors surrounded him. He was branded a heathen, called a wild boar and denounced as the devil incarnate. Martin grew tired of the unreasonable hatred of his enemies and constant death threats. Adding to his misery was his poor health.

His eyes lost their glow and his pace slowed to a crawl. A deep depression settled within him. Friends tried to encourage him, but he was too weary to listen to their counsel.

Katie decided it was time to act. He heard her wails the moment he entered the house. He discovered her dressed in mourning clothes, too lost in grief to even notice him.

"Who died, Katie?" he cried. "Who died?"

She finally quit sobbing enough to gasp, "Oh, Martin! God is dead! I can't bear it, for all His work is overthrown!"

Martin's face flushed in anger. "That is utter blasphemy, Katherina!" he raged.

Her sobs stopped and her voice grew stern. "Martin, you have been going around acting as if God is dead, as if God is no longer here to keep us. So I thought I ought to put on mourning to keep you company in your great bereavement."

Martin Luther got back to work.

Luther was 47 years old when he became totally disgusted with his complacent congregation. He decided to go on strike. Instead of his usual Sunday sermon, Luther announced, "I refuse to preach to you. You remain godless. It annoys me to keep preaching to you. When you mend your ways, I will return to my pulpit."

They mended.

He returned.

Charles H. Spurgeon said of Martin Luther: "...he was by no means of the weaker sort. His great spirit was often in seventh heaven of exultation, and as frequently on the borders of despair."

Charles Spurgeon said of himself while praying, "Lord, end my winter, and let my spring begin. I cannot with all my longing raise my soul out of her death and dullness, but all things are possible with Thee."

Spurgeon spoke of the critics who take out their penknives to gore and gash and added, "As it is recorded that David, in the heat of battle, waxed faint, so it may be written of all of the servants of the Lord. Fits of depression come over the most of us."

He also stated, "For my part, I am quite willing to be eaten by dogs for the next fifty years; but the more distant future shall vindicate me."

Today Spurgeon is referred to as "The Prince of Preachers." During his lifetime, he was often castigated—even despised—for his unyielding stance on crucial matters of Biblical principle. John F. MacArthur, Jr. said of Spurgeon: "His willingness to stand firm in the face of such hostility is the key to Spurgeon's real greatness."

It should encourage every pastor to know that he is not alone. David Wilkerson wrote about the ministers' gatherings he holds throughout Africa, South America, and Central America. Pastors there work a secular job to support

themselves while pastoring. He says they are discouraged
and wounded.

Chapter 7

The Beloved Wolf

Many pastors in America are not only discouraged and wounded; they are quitting. We all have heard at least one pastor say: "I quit! I don't have to put up with this! I'm going to sell cars...shoes...refrigerators...insurance... anything but this!"

If you have been called by God to work in His field, don't quit. When God calls a messenger, it is a calling without repentance. God expects His messengers to run the race straight into heaven—our one and only finish line.

A man called to service by God will trust God to supply his needs. He will follow the example left by Jesus. He will lay down his life daily for the sheep God has entrusted to His care.

Only hirelings quit. A hireling works only for a paycheck.

Jesus said, "he that is an hireling, and not the shepherd, whose own the sheep are not, **seeth the wolf coming**, and leaveth the sheep, and fleeth: and the wolf catcheth them, and scattereth the sheep. The hireling fleeth, because he is an hireling, and careth not for the sheep." *John 10:12-13*

When the wolf enters a church, he comes for one purpose—to eat sheep. Every sheep and every lamb is vulnerable to his attack.

Paul warned us about these times. "For I know this, that after my departing shall grievous wolves enter in among you, not sparing the flock."

Wolves.

They dress up in sheep's clothing. They work like sheep do, sing in the choir with the sheep, outwardly look like sheep, smell like sheep, bleat like sheep and act like sheep. And the sheep befriend the wolves who look just like them.

But one day, the shepherd sees the teeth of a wolf under the mask. Because of his love for the defenseless sheep, he attacks the wolf.

The bleating of the sheep join in a loud cry:

"Our pastor has attacked a sheep! What is wrong with our pastor?"

The pastor says, "This is a bad wolf that has come to eat you."

The congregation says, "This is a sheep. You are the wolf!"

The shepherd stays and endures the onslaught against him. But the hireling gives up, runs from the church and his ungrateful sheep. He may have battled wolves for years, but suddenly he has had it. The sheep, deceived by the costume that disguises the wolf, inevitably pity the wolf. Thus, the sheep become easy prey. The wolf devours them, one by one.

If the shepherd stays in the church to protect his sheep, the wolf leaves. But invariably, some of the sheep will follow the wolf out the door.

The only reason a pastor will remain with his flock during these times is because he truly cares for God's sheep.

"The hireling fleeth, because he is an hireling, and **careth not for the sheep**."

A pastor, called of God, will stay and endure the criticism from the flock for dealing with the wolf. He stays because there are precious, beloved sheep under his care that he loves so much he will sacrifice his own life for them.

Smite the Shepherd

Enemies of the church know how to destroy a flock. The formula they use is revealed to us in the Bible:

"Smite the shepherd, and the sheep shall be scattered." *Zechariah 13:7; Matthew 26:31; Mark 14:27*

Smite the shepherd....

Smite means to **beat, smack, torment, hit, strike, afflict, plague, grieve, or distress**.

Every shepherd will be smitten—lied about, talked about, criticized, hated, and ridiculed. Some shepherds will not endure these grievous times. When they leave their flocks, the sheep will be scattered. Many sheep will not be found in any church within six months.

The constant attack is unleashed against the shepherd.

If *a sheep* is attacked, *a sheep* will be destroyed.

If *a shepherd* is destroyed, *a flock* will be destroyed.

If *a pastor* is destroyed, *a church* will be destroyed.

Pastors do not enjoy being smitten. However, every pastor who is called by God to care for God's flock will be smitten—over and over and over again.

Jesus warns us that we "...resist not evil: but whosoever shall __*smite thee*__ on thy right cheek, turn to him the other also." *Matthew 5:39*

The temptation is to smite back.

The temptation is to quit being a target for the smiters.

The temptation is to quit pastoring.

Turning the cheek means to make ourselves vulnerable to be smitten again. In other words, we stay in the ministry, knowing we will have to continuously endure being slapped.

Our Lord, the Good Shepherd, left us an Example.

"For even hereunto were ye called: because Christ also suffered for us, leaving us an example, that *ye should follow his steps*: Who did no sin, neither was guile found in his mouth: Who, when he was reviled, reviled not again; when he suffered, he threatened not; but committed himself to him that judgeth righteously." *I Peter 2:21-23*

The wolves gathered together to mock and ridicule Jesus even as His blood poured from His tortured body. He could have left the cross. If He had, the entire human race would be doomed. He chose instead to remain on the cross and endure the scorn and the shame.

Have you entered the ministry to proclaim the name of Jesus Christ? Do you intend to invite your listeners to the foot of the cross to have their sins washed away? The scorners are still gathered there, mocking, ridiculing, despising, jeering. Today they despise the servants of Jesus.

"Proud and haughty scorner is his name, who dealeth in proud wrath." *Proverbs 21:24*

You can walk away. But your choice may result in many souls going into eternity unsaved.

The great Apostle Paul told us about his life of endurance.

"I am...in labours more abundant, in stripes above measure, in prisons more frequent, in deaths oft...five times received I forty stripes save one. Thrice was I beaten with rods, once was I stoned, thrice I suffered shipwreck, a night and a day I have been in the deep; in journeyings often, in perils of waters, in perils of robbers, in perils by mine own countrymen, in perils by the heathen, in perils in the city, in perils in the wilderness, in perils in the sea, in perils among false brethren; in weariness and painfulness, in watchings often, in hunger and thirst, in fastings often, in cold and nakedness. Beside those things that are without, **that which cometh upon me daily, the care of all the churches.**" *II Corinthians 11:23-28*

Paul summed up his commitment just before he was killed: "***I have fought***... ***I have finished***...***I have kept.***"

After we receive the warning about the wolves entering in among the church, Paul adds: "**Also of your own selves shall men arise, speaking perverse things, to draw away disciples after them**." *Acts 20:30*

Every pastor has seen it time and again. Someone rises up out of the congregation, seeking a following. It matters not how long the pastor has loved the sheep and cared for them.

One who seeks glory for himself rises up out of the congregation, desiring sheep to follow him, rather than the shepherd. Invariably, some of the sheep will turn on their pastor and follow another out the door of the church.

The sheep seldom even listen to the message spoken by the one they are following. (The message usually consists of one theme: "The pastor is bad.") The sheep don't care that they are following one who is "speaking perverse things." The sheep don't realize that the one they are following cares nothing about protecting them from harm. The sheep do not discern the glory-seeker's self-centered motives.

"Of your own selves shall men arise...**to draw away disciples _after them_**...."

The glory-seeker seeks disciples for himself, not for Jesus. As the pastor views the exodus, he feels rejected by the sheep he has cared for and loved. He grieves for the sheep. He prays the sheep that have left will find a shepherd who will love them enough to watch over their souls.

Chapter 8

Seeking a Miracle

"And a great multitude followed him, ***because they saw his miracles*** which he did on them that were diseased."
John 6:2

Just as people followed Jesus for different reasons, people come to church for various reasons. Some come during their time of need. When they no longer need the pastor's prayers for a miracle, the pastor's counsel, the church's financial help, the use of the sanctuary for a wedding or a funeral, letters sent to a prisoner, or visits to a hospital bed, they leave the church. The excuse for leaving is never, "I only came because I needed something from the church. I left when I got it!"

Their excuse will more likely be that the pastor is rude, unfriendly, did or said something they didn't agree with, or didn't do or say something they thought he should have done or said. The mean pastor is blamed for their self-centeredness.

Jesus looked over the multitude who followed Him and said: "Ye seek me, not because ye saw the miracles, but because ye did eat of the loaves, and were filled. Labour not for the meat which perisheth, but for that meat which endureth unto everlasting life...He that eateth my flesh, and drinketh my blood, dwelleth in me, and I in him. This is that bread which came down from heaven: not as your fathers did eat manna, and are dead: he that eateth of this bread shall live forever. From that time **many of his disciples went back, and walked no more with him**."
John 6:26-27, 56, 58, 66

This crowd did not seek a Savior who could give them eternal life. They came only for a meal. Food and fellowship were sufficient. They had no desire to hear what He could give them after they died. What did He have for them **now?** When their stomachs were full and the conversation changed to spiritual things, they left.

The crowds today are no different. Among them are the ones who drift into the church for food and fellowship. When the talk gets too spiritual, they leave.   Why stay? Their stomachs are full. **"Ye did eat of the loaves, and were filled...."**

Jesus said of the crowd who came for their miracle or their meal: "...many believed in his name, when they saw the miracles which he did. But Jesus did not commit himself unto them, because he knew all men." *John 2:23-24*

John knew why they were part of His crowd. He did not commit *(obligate)* Himself unto them because He knew that they did not commit themselves unto Him. The following verse says, **"...*he knew what was in man.*"**

Unfortunately, pastors often do commit themselves unto these people. They commit their friendship, their love, their trust, and their time. When one walks away from what the pastor believed was a mutual friendship, the pastor feels rejected. Each time this happens, he finds it a little harder to commit himself to someone else.

Seeking a Rest

Some come into the church and dedicate themselves wholeheartedly to the work. Pastors are thrilled that someone has come to labor rather than to rest; to give, rather than to take. The pastor begins to rely on these committed laborers who support the church physically, spiritually and financially.

But some of these dedicated workers stop working long enough to look around at members who are doing nothing. They wonder if they are regarded as "The Drudge." When there is work to be done, they are the first ones that are called upon, while the others sit idly by. They are seldom even thanked. Their hearts fill with resentment and they suddenly feel very tired.

A recliner and the remote look extremely inviting. "Family time" suddenly becomes vitally important. The boat, the golf course, and relaxation—anything and everything begins to look more appealing than working in the church!

The worker doesn't know quite how to handle the situation. He can't admit the truth to the pastor and congregation, or even to himself.

The truth would be, "You expect me to do all the work, while most of you do nothing. So I quit. I have decided to backslide with the rest of you."

Since he can't do that, he leaves the church. People ask him why he left. He can't reveal his real reason for leaving. His only solution is to point his accusing finger toward the pastor. He surely did or said something wrong. He can blame him! (This is a tactic as old as the Garden of Eden. "Eve made me do it!" "The devil made me do it!") Now it is, "The bad pastor made me do it!" He finds another church where he can slip in, sit for an hour on Sunday morning, and be appreciated for just showing up. He has left the pastor with his remaining congregation, now looking at him a little more skeptically, wondering if the accusations they have heard about him are true.

And the pastor's pace becomes just a little slower—and the recliner and the boat look pretty appealing to him too.

Chapter 9

Don't Give Up

Thousands of pastors are giving up the fight. Thousands are not finishing their race.

Jesus warned us "...because iniquity shall abound, the love of many shall wax cold." *Matthew 24:12*

Sin surrounds us today, nearly crushing us. But the love that Christ placed in us for dying, hurting humanity does not have to turn to ice. We do not have to...

Quit loving rebellious sheep.
Quit loving sinners who need salvation.
Quit loving sheep who cuddle hungry wolves.
Begin to love ourselves more than our sheep.

Jesus said, "...the good shepherd giveth his life for the sheep." *John 10:11*

The good shepherd gives his time, strength, love, forgiveness, and ***even his reputation.***

Lies destroy our reputations. If a pastor expects to have a distinguished reputation and be looked up to and respected by all, he has not read the Bible!

The Bible instructs us to "Let this mind be in you,

which was also in Christ Jesus: Who...***made himself of no reputation***." *Philippians 2:7*

Jesus was called mad, devil-possessed, a liar, a law-breaker and a blasphemer.

> Some ***told*** lies about Jesus.
> And some ***believed*** lies about Jesus.
> There are always tongues willing to ***tell*** lies.
> And there are always ears willing to ***listen to*** lies.

Unfortunately, there are always waiting ears, anxious to hear and ready to believe every lie that is told about a pastor.

(If we believed even half the lies that were told about us, we would not be able to live with ourselves.)

Jesus said, "Blessed are ye, when men shall revile you, and persecute you, and shall ***say all manner of evil against you falsely***, for my sake. ***Rejoice, and be exceeding glad***: for great is your reward in heaven: for so persecuted they the prophets which were before you." *Matthew 5:11-12*

It is hard to feel blessed when we are lied about. It is extremely hard to rejoice during these times. And it is nearly impossible to be glad—not just glad—but ***exceeding*** glad when we hear the lies being told about us.

Exceeding glad means: ***Really glad! Very glad! Extremely glad!***

People lied about God's messengers before our time, and people will lie about us. There is only one way to stay happy in the midst of this. "Rejoice, and be exceeding glad: ***for great is your reward in heaven....***" *Matthew 5:12*

Our reward is:

Not now. It comes later.
Not here. We receive it in heaven.

We must keep our hearts in heaven and our eyes on Jesus! Paul told us we must keep looking to Jesus to keep going.

"Looking unto Jesus the author and finisher of our faith; who for the joy that was set before him endured the cross, despising the shame, and is set down at the right hand of the throne of God. For **consider him** that endured such contradiction of sinners against himself, lest **_ye be wearied and faint in your minds_."** *Hebrews 12:2-3*

Do you see what happens if we quit looking at Jesus? Our minds will faint! We will quit! We will fall away! We will depart from the faith!

"Whatsoever ye do, do it heartily, **as to the Lord**, and not unto men; knowing that of the Lord ye shall receive the reward of the inheritance: for **ye serve the Lord Christ**." *Colossians 3:23-24*

Don't Fall!

"A thousand shall fall at thy side, and ten thousand at thy right hand; but it shall not come nigh thee." *Psalm 91:7*

Eighteen thousand pastors may walk away from the call of God every year, but _you_ don't have to be in the crowd!

"Let no man deceive you by any means: for that day shall not come, except there come *a falling away* first...." *II Thessalonians 2:3*

Have you already fallen? Then get back up! We need you! The harvest is ripe! The laborers are few! "For a just man falleth seven times, and riseth up again...." *Proverbs 24:16*

Don't Depart!

"Now the Spirit speaketh expressly, that in the latter times *some shall depart* from the faith, giving heed to seducing spirits, and doctrines of devils." *I Timothy 4:1*

Yes, some are departing from the faith. But you don't have to be one who walks away from your faith in God and His call on your life!

Press On!

Paul wrote: "I *press* toward the mark for the prize of the high calling of God in Christ Jesus." *Philippians 3:14*

Pressing on means to keep on going, even though pressure bombards us! Many are quitting under the pressures of the ministry. You don't have to be one!

Keep Running!

"Wherefore seeing we also are compassed about with so great a cloud of witnesses, let us lay aside every weight, and the sin which doth so easily beset us, and **let us run** with patience the race that is set before us." *Hebrews 12:1*

Take off the weights. Get rid of the sins. Run!

Don't Faint!

"And let us not be weary in well doing: for in due season we shall reap, if we faint not." *Galatians 6:9*

Don't faint! We need you!

Do you think you are not needed? We hear many pastors refer to their "small churches."   As a God-ordained pastor, you are part of a blood-bought eternal church.

It was founded by our Lord Jesus Christ.

The gates of hell itself will not prevail against God's triumphant church!

It is a victorious church!

It has endured an onslaught from the hosts of darkness for twenty centuries!

Yet God's church continues to win souls, evangelize nations, feed the hungry, minister to the imprisoned, clothe the naked, visit the sick, care for the widows and orphans, and raise a standard of righteousness in the world. The devil and the world despise our standard of righteousness, but we continue to fight, armed with God's Word, our sword.

The devil would like nothing more than to stop **every word** from **every mouth** of **every servant** of the living God.

The Word of God is the sword that God has placed in the hand of His church. It is spoken by the messengers of God. It is our only weapon. We can't let Satan disarm us! We must fight for Jesus Christ, our righteous King, even unto death.

"For…it pleased God by the foolishness of **preaching** to save them that believe." *I Corinthians 1:21*

You are a pastor of the church founded by Jesus Christ! Jesus was sent from heaven to found this church! Jesus purchased this church with His own blood! Jesus is returning to earth to receive this church into heaven! He has made **you** a pastor of this great church! **Your work** is vital!

Churches held in homes were mentioned in the Bible. They were never identified as small churches! Here are three:

1. "Aquila and Priscilla salute you much in the Lord, with the church **that is in their house.**" *I Corinthians 16:19*

2. "And to our beloved Apphia, and Archippus our fellowsoldier, and **to the church in thy house.**" *Philemon 1:2*

3. "Salute the brethren which are in Laodicea, and Nymphas, **and the church which is in his house.**" *Colossians 4:15*

The Bible does not refer to little churches, medium churches and mega churches! We are all part of that glorious church that Christ loved and died for. Every pastor, no matter the size of his flock or the capacity of his sheep shed, is needed to do the work of our Lord.

- There were only 120 men and women in the upper room.

- The reformation began as Martin Luther taught just a few students at Wittenberg.

- John Wesley found Christ at a back alley prayer meeting at Aldersgate.

- Charles H. Spurgeon joined the race in a tiny chapel.

- Jesus chose twelve disciples to follow Him.

- Jesus appeared to a crowd of five hundred after His resurrection, but only one hundred twenty showed up to wait for His promise to send the Holy Spirit upon them.

- Noah faithfully warned his generation, but salvaged only his family from God's judgment.

- Peter described Lot as a righteous man who was daily vexed with seeing and hearing the filthy lifestyle and conversation. Yet he didn't even save his whole family. Only two corrupt daughters were salvaged.

Don't judge your worth by the size of your congregation!

Don't judge your worth by the grumbling and murmuring of your congregation!

Judge your worth by your obedience to the voice of your King!

If you faithfully pastor a flock in your house, you are fulfilling your calling. Our job is not to fill pews with people. ***Our ministry is to fill people with God!*** If every pastor simply remains faithful to the flock God has given to him to pastor, this job will get done!

Chapter 10

Crucial Days

This is not a day to give in to discouragement. We are living in perilous times. Every God-ordained voice needs to be heard in this crucial day.

Families are broken.
Children are neglected.
Minds are perverted.
The Bible is ridiculed.
Churches are locked on Sunday evenings.
The name of Jesus is blasphemed.
Prayer is outlawed.
The Ten Commandments are ripped off walls.
Sunday Schools are closing.
Violence is increasing.
Sodomy is accepted.

This is the day we were warned about: "Let us consider one another to provoke unto love and to good works: not forsaking the assembling of ourselves together, as the manner of some is; but exhorting one another: and **_so much the more_**, as ye see the day approaching." *Hebrews 10:24-25*

Unfortunately, the church is not meeting **_more_** as we see the day of Christ's return approaching. It is meeting **_less!_**

Pastor, if you are born-again, blood-bought and God-called—we need you! Don't give up! If a church member has attacked you, remember what Paul did when the viper attacked him. He shook it off! The islanders and 275 men from his ship watched, waiting for Paul to swell up and die. He didn't. He did what we need to do. We need to shake off the serpent and go on about God's business. The parishioners will eventually come to their senses and realize we are not going to swell up and die.

There will always be the Jezebels trying to kill the Elijahs. Rather than letting them destroy us, we need to look at their endings.

Jezebel was torn apart by dogs.

Elijah was picked up in a chariot of fire and ushered into heaven in style.

Jezebels have one purpose in mind—to kill the man of God. Oh, today's Jezebel may not gather up assassins to kill him. Today's Jezebels will most likely not even threaten the pastor to his face. But the spirit will be the same—and the purpose will be the same—to kill the ministry and stop the words of God's messenger. **_Don't let them do it._**

When we feel the pressure closing in around us, we need to pray the prayer Uncle Bud Robinson prayed:

"Oh, Lord, give me a back-bone as big as a saw log, and ribs like the sleepers under the church floor; put iron shoes on me, and galvanized breeches. And give me a rhinoceros hide for a skin, and hang a wagon load of determination up in the gable-end of my soul, and help me to sign the contract to fight the devil as long as I've got a fist, and bite him as long as I've got a tooth and then gum him till I die. All this I ask for Christ's sake, AMEN!"

You may have to flee from one place and settle in another, but continue to proclaim the Word of the Lord wherever you land.

It's no shame to flee from persecutors. Jesus escaped from angry mobs. Paul was let down a wall in a basket by the disciples to escape his persecutors. The early Christians fled from Jerusalem. Elijah fled from Jezebel and her team of hit men. But each one of them kept speaking the Word of the Lord. Not one threw away his sword and retreated from the battle.

We need every voice who will fearlessly speak the Word of God. We must show "to the generation to come the praises of the LORD, and his strength, and his wonderful works that he hath done." *Psalm 78:4*

Will we allow our voices to be silenced by the enemy of the gospel?

Dare we risk hearing our world cry, "The harvest is past, the summer is ended, and we are not saved." *Jeremiah 8:20*

Chapter 11

May God Strengthen Your Heart

When people attack a shepherd, his heart is smitten and wounded.

David wrote: "My heart is smitten, and withered like grass. My heart is wounded within me." *Psalm 102:4, 109:22*

Don't be disheartened because of your persecutors.

Would you rather be the liar, or the lied about?

Would you rather be the persecutor, or the persecuted?

Would you rather be the slapper, or the slapped?

Which would you rather hear Jesus say? "Depart from me, ye that work iniquity," or "Well done, thou good and faithful servant!"

God's Marching Orders

Here are the marching orders for God's ministers: "I charge thee therefore before God, and the Lord Jesus Christ, who shall judge the quick and the dead at his appearing and his kingdom;"

"Preach the word; be instant in season, out of season; reprove, rebuke, exhort with all longsuffering and doctrine."

"For the time will come when they will not endure sound doctrine; but after their own lusts shall they heap to themselves teachers, having itching ears; and they shall turn away their ears from the truth, and shall be turned unto fables."

"But watch thou in all things, endure afflictions, do the work of an evangelist, make full proof of thy ministry." *II Timothy 4:1-5*

Follow Jesus! He said, "I have glorified thee on the earth: **_I have finished the work which thou gavest me to do_.**" *John 17:4*

Don't just **_begin_** your work! **_Finish it!_**

Chapter 12

Leave the Results to God

The **works** of your ministry are up to you.

The **results** of your ministry are up to the Lord.

God called Ezekiel to speak His Word. It was up to him to speak for God whether anyone listened or not. God warned him when He sent him to the crowds that no one would listen to him. Because Ezekiel was faithful, those who listened to his message will be without excuse on their day of judgment.

God sent Ezekiel into the ministry with these words: "Son of man, I send thee to the children of Israel, to a rebellious nation that hath rebelled against me: they and their fathers have transgressed against me, even unto this very day. For they are impudent children and stiffhearted. I do send thee unto them; and thou shalt say unto them. Thus saith the Lord GOD."

"And they, **whether they will hear, or whether they will forbear**, (for they are a rebellious house,) **yet shall know that there hath been a prophet among them.**"

"And thou, son of man, be not afraid of them, neither be afraid of their words, though briers and thorns be with thee, and thou dost dwell among scorpions: be not afraid of their words, nor be dismayed at their looks, though they be a rebellious house. And ***thou shalt speak my words unto them, whether they will hear, or whether they will forbear***: for they are most rebellious. But thou, son of man, hear what I say unto thee; ***be not thou rebellious*** like that rebellious house: ***open thy mouth***, and eat that I give thee." *Ezekiel 2:3-8*

Having a rebellious congregation gives a pastor no excuse to become a rebellious messenger. Our responsibility is to speak the Word of the Lord, whether or not anyone chooses to listen and obey it.

God called Jeremiah with this command: "Thou therefore gird up thy loins, and arise, and speak unto them all that I command thee: be not dismayed at their faces, lest I confound thee before them.

"For, behold, I have made thee this day a defenced city, and an iron pillar, and brazen walls...and ***they shall fight against thee***; but ***they shall not prevail*** against thee; for I am with thee, saith the LORD, to deliver thee." *Jeremiah 1:17-19*

Who would fight against Jeremiah as he preached? Unfortunately, it was Israel, the people chosen by God— the congregation God gave to Jeremiah.

The very sheep God calls us to shepherd may be the ones who fight against us. But even that is no excuse to give up.

Chapter 13

A Word of Warning

The devil cannot stand it when God's messengers are praised. On the heels of every victory is a battle.

Jesus was surrounded by people praising Him on Palm Sunday. **On Friday, they were calling for His execution.**

Elijah prayed fire down from heaven and the people worshiped God. The false prophets were destroyed. **Jezebel got the news, called for his head, and Elijah ran for his life.**

Moses held his rod over the sea, and the waters were parted. The enemy was overthrown. The Israelites rejoiced, praised, shouted, and danced. **Three days later they needed water and accused Moses of bringing them into the desert to kill them all of thirst.**

David killed Goliath. The women sang: "Saul hath slain his thousands, and David his ten thousands!" **King Saul hurled his javelin at David, hoping to pin him to the wall with it.**

Paul was on a ship going down. An angel appeared with a message. Paul gave orders and all 276 men were saved. They swam and floated to an island where the natives received them with kindness. ***The island was crowded with the 276 men from the ship and all the natives. A viper chose to attach itself to just one man…the apostle Paul.***

When you are being praised—brace yourself. The enemy will be waiting for his opportunity. Be armed, prayed up, and ready for him.

"The devil is come down **unto you**, having great wrath, because he knoweth that he hath but a short time. Submit yourselves therefore to God. Resist the devil, and he will flee from you." *Revelation 12:12; James 4:7*

Toughen Up!

Paul wrote about how we must be when times get tough: "Finally, my brethren, **be strong** in the Lord, and in the power of his might. Therefore, my beloved brethren, be ye steadfast (tough), unmovable, always abounding in the work of the Lord, forasmuch as ye know that your labour is not in vain in the Lord." *Ephesians 6:10; I Corinthians 15:58*

Abide!

During our times of discouragement and temptation to quit, God has often reminded us of "our special verse." It is our call to tough it out in the hard times. It is found in an unlikely place—nestled in the Christmas story. Here it is:

"And there were in the same country shepherds ***abiding*** in the field, ***keeping watch over their flock by night***." *Luke 2:8*

> It is nighttime.
> The world is growing darker by the minute.
> Wolves abound.
> Danger lurks.
> God's precious sheep are vulnerable.

Shepherds need to ***abide*** in the field, keeping watch over the flocks that our great Shepherd has entrusted to our care. Abide means to ***remain; stay; persevere; or endure***.

Jesus left the splendors of heaven to come down to a perverted, faithless human race. Thank God He ***stayed*** until His work was done. His cry yet echoes from Calvary's hill: ***"It is finished."***

Abraham, referred to in the New Testament as a faithful man, the father of us all, was promised a land for his descendants. When he died, he held title to only one small piece of land—a burial plot for his beloved wife. ***Yet today***—today Abraham's descendants possess the Promised Land!

"For all the promises of God in him are yea, and in him Amen, unto the glory of God by us." *II Corinthians 1:20*

"For the vision is yet for an appointed time, but at the end it shall speak, and not lie: though it tarry, wait for it; because it will surely come, it will not tarry." *Habakkuk 2:3*

> What God said, He has done.
> What God says, He will do.

Hold on to your faith!

Hold on to your calling!

Finish the work God has given you to do!

Paul kept the faith, even as he wrote from his prison cell to the church he longed to be with: "But I trust in the Lord Jesus to send Timotheus shortly unto you, that I also may be of good comfort, when I know your state. For I **have no man likeminded**, who will naturally care for your state. For **all seek their own**, not the things which are Jesus Christ's." *Philippians 2:19-21*

Paul, called by God to do a mighty work, a powerful teacher of the Word of God, looked at his self-centered leaders, and wrote from his jail cell: "At least I have Timothy."

Moses stood by, as God killed a good portion of his congregation because of their rebellion. The same congregation, who had walked across dry land in the middle of the Red Sea, ate food delivered to them from heaven and drank water from a rock that became a river...now murmured...and complained...and moaned...and rebelled... and doubted...and grumbled.

Through it all, God expects us to remain with our flocks. God refers to His pastors as gifts to His church. (Few on earth will refer to their pastor as a gift—but it is God's favor we seek, not man's!)

"Wherefore he saith, When he ascended up on high, he led captivity captive, and **_gave gifts_** unto men...and **_he gave_ some, apostles; and some, prophets; and some, evangelists; and some, pastors and teachers**; for the perfecting of the saints, for the work of the ministry, for the edifying of the body of Christ: till we all come in the unity of the faith, and of the knowledge of the Son of God, unto a perfect man, unto the measure of the stature of the fullness of Christ." *Ephesians 4:8-13*

God told the Israelites: "And I, behold, I have taken your brethren the Levites from among the children of Israel: **to you they are given as a gift** for the LORD, to do the service of the tabernacle of the congregation." *Numbers 18:6*

Jesus left a message to each of the seven churches in the book of Revelation. He delivered it through His beloved disciple, John. Listen to the way he addressed each message:

1. "Unto the angel of the church of Ephesus...."
2. "Unto the angel of the church in Smyrna...."
3. "To the angel of the church in Pergamos...."
4. "Unto the angel of the church in Thyatira...."
5. "Unto the angel of the church in Sardis...."
6. "To the angel of the church in Philadelphia...."
7. "Unto the angel of the church of Laodicea...."

To the angel...to <u>my messenger</u>...to <u>the shepherd</u> in My church who leads My flock....

How can we let discouragement overtake our joy when we serve such a Master? His grace is so amazing that He refers to His messengers as ***gifts*** to His church! His mercy is so awesome that He refers to the pastors of the seven churches as His angels (messengers)! His love is so wonderful that no other opinions should matter to us in the least!

Chapter 14

The Encouragers

We have dwelt on the discouraging times in these pages and neglected the glorious and rewarding times of the ministry for one reason. This is a book written to encourage pastors who are tempted to quit the ministry. It is the discouragements, the disappointments, the complainers, the betrayers, and the haters that the enemy uses to wear us down.

When Moses turned the reigns of his ministry over to young Joshua, he asked the congregation to encourage him and strengthen him. In nearly every congregation there are the helpers; the strengtheners; the thankful; the cheerful; the encouragers; those who love us in spite of us. There are the Aarons and the Hurs who hold up the hands of Moses in the heat of the battle.

How is it that the grumblers stand out in a crowd, while the encouragers just fade into the background during the rough times? Could it be we pastors are guilty of focusing on the wrong thing? What do you see in this picture?

Is your answer, "A black dot"? We often look at the one black dot, rather than all the white that surrounds it.

Jesus ministered in the midst of a mob who screamed for His death, tried to push Him over a cliff, gathered rocks to stone Him, called Him a liar and a blasphemer, accused Him of being devil-possessed, pronounced Him insane and finally succeeded in nailing Him to a cross.

Why did He continue?

"Looking unto Jesus the author and finisher of our faith; who **_for the joy that was set before him_** endured...." *Hebrews 12:2*

He focused on the joy that was set before Him....

"Take heed therefore unto yourselves, and to all **_the flock_**, over the which the Holy Ghost hath made you overseers, to feed the church of God, which **_he hath purchased with his own blood._**" *Acts 20:28*

"I am the good shepherd: the good shepherd giveth his life for the sheep." *John 10:11*

Jesus endured because He was purchasing His flock, the church, His beloved bride....

"And I, John, saw the holy city, new Jerusalem, coming down from God out of heaven, prepared **_as a bride adorned for her husband_**. And I heard a great voice out of heaven saying, Behold, the tabernacle of God is with men, and he will dwell with them, and they shall be his people, and God himself shall be with them, and be their God. And God shall wipe away all tears from their eyes; and there shall be no more death, neither sorrow, nor crying, neither shall there be any more pain: for the former things are passed away.

And he that sat upon the throne said, Behold, I make all things new. And he said unto me, Write: for these words are true and faithful." *Revelation 21:2-5*

The bride, loved by our King so much that He purchased her with His own blood, was **the joy** that was set before Him. And for the JOY that was set before Him, Christ endured.

In Light of Eternity

A man lived a life of wealth and health for 70 years. His days were filled with loyal friends, constant love and joy. As he neared death, his friends and family gathered around him. They were shocked to hear this bitter complaint pour from his dying body.

"I have had seventy wonderful years—except for eight hours one dark day. I suffered a bad headache. My neighbor was rude to me. My dog snarled at me. My wife refused to greet me with a smile when she brought my breakfast. My son was disobedient and rebellious."

The man's final words were full of resentment. "Those eight hours of my life were dreadful."

It would be utterly ridiculous for a man to complain about having troubles for eight hours of his life and forget about the 613,192 hours he was trouble free!

Let us consider this story in the light of eternity.

We will liken the eight hours of trouble to our lifetime on earth.

If trials and troubles fill our entire lifetime, what is that, in comparison to eternity?

Will we spend our first 10,000 years in heaven, complaining bitterly: "I had trouble while I was living on earth. People didn't like me. Some even told lies about me. I was slandered."

Doesn't it strike you as ridiculous that we ungrateful people dare to complain about troubles in our life when we are promised **ETERNITY** trouble free?

"For what is your life? It is even a vapour, that appeareth for a little time, and then vanisheth away." *James 4:14*

No wonder the apostle Paul could say, "But what things were gain to me, those I counted loss for Christ. Yea doubtless, and I count all things but loss for the excellency of the knowledge of Christ Jesus my Lord: for whom I have suffered the loss of all things, and do count them but dung, that I may win Christ." *Philippians 3:7-8*

Those Miserable Black Dots

There will be no black dot to mar the bride when all our work is finished.

Today the black dots are visible. They are not only visible to us; they are also visible to God.

Listen, as God describes the spots and blemishes: "The Lord knoweth how to deliver the godly out of temptations, and to reserve the unjust unto the day of judgment to be punished: but chiefly them that walk after the flesh in the lust of uncleanness, and despise government. Presumptuous **(arrogant)** are they, self-willed, they are not afraid to speak evil of dignities.

"Whereas angels, which are greater in power and might, bring not railing accusation against them before the Lord. But these, as natural brute beasts, made to be taken and destroyed, speak evil of the things that they understand not; and shall utterly perish in their own corruption; and shall receive the reward of unrighteousness, as they that count it pleasure to riot in the day time.

"Spots they are and blemishes, sporting themselves with their own deceivings *while they feast with you."* *II Peter 2:10-13*

The spots and blemishes may feast with the church today. However, no spot or blemish will enter heaven.

"...Christ also loved the church, and gave himself for it; that he might sanctify and cleanse it with the washing of water by the word, that he might present it to himself a glorious church, *not having spot*, or wrinkle, or any such thing; but that it should be holy and **without blemish**." *Ephesians 5:25-27*

Jesus will receive His church into heaven, and it will be a glorious church.

The spots that show up so clearly today will be absent tomorrow.

God left us this glimpse of heaven:

"And a voice came out of the throne, saying, Praise our God, all ye his servants, and ye that fear him, both small and great. And I heard as it were the voice of a great multitude, and as the voice of many waters, and as the voice of mighty thunderings, saying, Alleluia: for the Lord God omnipotent reigneth."

"Let us be glad and rejoice, and give honour to him: for the marriage of the Lamb is come, and his wife hath made herself ready. And to her was granted that she should be arrayed in fine linen, clean and white: for the fine linen is the righteousness of saints. And he saith unto me, Write, blessed are they which are called unto the marriage supper of the Lamb. And he saith unto me, These are the true sayings of God." *Revelation 19:5-9*

Until that glorious day, we must continue to heed our Lord's words to us: "Watchman, what of the night? Watchman, what of the night?" *Isaiah 21:11*

Let us answer our Lord with this renewed commitment: "I must work the works of him that sent me, while it is day: the night cometh, when no man can work." *John 9:4*

Let us remember the blessings reserved for the faithful shepherds who stayed with their flock during the night hours that first Christmas.

The angel of the Lord came upon them!
The glory of the Lord shone round about them!
They heard God's choir in the skies!
They looked upon Jesus!

"Let the LORD, the God of the spirits of all flesh, set a man over the congregation, which may go out before them, and which may go in before them, and which may lead them out, and which may bring them in; that the congregation of the LORD be not as sheep which have no shepherd." Numbers 27:16-17

I Climbed the Mountain

The night was black
Rain was pelting the mountain
Where the little lamb lay.
I looked up just as
A flashing spear of lightning
Lit the night sky.

And I saw the Shepherd,
Balancing on a ledge,
Holding onto a branch with one hand,
Reaching down with the other.
Just a quick glimpse,
And the light was gone.

Darkness seemed especially black
Until the next flash revealed the lamb.
Its head was buried in its wool
And it was trembling,
Aware only of its own misery,
the Shepherd unheeded.

Thunders crashed through the mountains.
I waited anxiously to see the next scene.
But then I saw the Shepherd.
And I trembled. His eyes no longer
Looked upon the lamb.
They were fixed on me.

I knew instantly what He
Expected me to do.
Me! I was no mountain climber!
The mountain was huge, menacing.
I trembled with fear
Just thinking about the climb!
Failure would mean my doom!

Even in darkness I could feel His eyes—
Boring into my own.
I could not remain a spectator.
He was forcing me
To become part of the scene.

I vibrated with dread.
How dare He force me
To get involved?
The sheerness of the mountain wall;
Raging winds, deafening thunder;
Streaks of lightning—I was terrified!

Must I sacrifice myself…
Just for a little lamb?
Didn't this Shepherd have enough lambs
Safely at home in His fold?
Why should I risk my life
On such a night as this?

The next flash of light
Revealed what I already knew.
His eyes were still piercing mine.

He was not going to let me
View this scene in peace.
I cautiously began to climb.

Grabbing a branch.
Waiting for the light to flash.
Finding a toehold here,
And a stepping stone there.
I got about halfway up
When I decided to quit.

I looked down only to see
That I couldn't descend.
I had no place to go.
So I just kept climbing.
Taking one small step at a time,
I at last reached the cowering lamb.

The Shepherd's hand was just above it.
It only took a small effort on my part
To span that small space between
The Shepherd's hand and His little lamb.
I watched as the lamb was safely
Cuddled to the heart of its Shepherd.

I heard the faint bleat of another lamb—
And another. Then another.
Wounded lambs. Lost lambs.
Dying lambs. Shivering lambs.
I forgot my fears, as I handed them up
To their waiting Shepherd.

He took each one tenderly.
Caressing, covering, warming them
In the folds of His garment.
I passed another to Him.
Watching and waiting to see
Him nestle it to Himself.

But I saw instead the Shepherd's face,
The sun had never shone as brightly.
He was smiling—smiling at me!
I felt myself being lifted then
Straight into the Shepherd's bosom,
Enfolded right next to His heart.

Nestled beside me were rescued lambs,
Quiet now, contented and safe.
The Shepherd spoke gently to me:
"Well done, My child! Well done!
You are a good and faithful servant.
Enter thou into the joy of the Lord."

Eternal Joy.
The Rescued Lambs.
The Smiling Shepherd.
The Everlasting Day.
The Forgotten Night.

**I am so glad
I climbed the mountain!**

CAROLYN WILDE

Chapter 15

Dwight L. Moody Deals With a Critic

Note: Everyone who serves God has his share of critics. Every decision is questioned, every comment is scrutinized, and every expression is examined. There is only one way to keep from getting criticized by the critics. Do nothing. As long as you are doing anything for our Master, you are subjecting yourself to opposition, criticism, hostility, hatred and rejection. Here is how Dwight L. Moody, one of the world's most successful evangelists, dealt with one of his critics.

By the time Dwight was 17, he had become a successful shoe salesman for Holton's Shoe Store. Moody accepted Christ in the back room of the shoe store through the guidance of his Sunday School teacher. Later, he became actively involved in the Plymouth Congregational Church in Chicago. As a layman, he began renting the church pews and filling them up with men and women whom he had invited.

He went on to become one of the world's greatest evangelists. But he never got away from his simple commitment and the memories of the first time he stood up to speak as a young man, when one of the deacons assured him that, in his opinion, he would serve God best by keeping still. Another critic praised Moody for his zeal but pleaded with him, saying that he should realize his limitations and not attempt to speak in public. "You make too many mistakes in grammar."

Moody patiently replied: "I know I make mistakes, and I lack many things, but I'm doing the best I can with what I've got." He then quietly looked at the man and searchingly inquired, "Look here, friend, you've got grammar enough. What are you doing with it for the Master?"

John Wesley's Shout of Relief

John Wesley wrote over 200 books, edited a magazine, compiled dictionaries in four languages, and composed a home medical handbook—all in his own handwriting! He traveled over 250,000 miles on horseback—the equivalent of riding ten times around the world along its equator. He preached more than 40,000 powerful sermons, some to crowds of over 20,000. Only eternity will reveal how many hundreds of thousands of souls were saved through John's committed life.

He was constantly heckled and jeered. He was riding along a dusty road one day when it occurred to him that three whole days had passed in which he had suffered no persecution! He was horrified. No bricks had been thrown. He had not even been bombarded with one egg!

He knew he was in trouble. He immediately stopped his horse with a shout and fell to his knees.

"My Lord," he cried. "Show me my fault! Am I backslidden? Have I sinned?"

A fellow on the other side of the hedge heard his prayer and recognized him.

"I'll fix that Methodist preacher," he said, picking up a brick and hurling it at him.

The brick fell short of its mark, but John, leaping to his feet, joyfully shouted, "Thank God! It's all right! I still have God's presence!"

George Whitefield's Consolation

George Whitefield, sometimes referred to as "The Lightning Rod of the Great Awakening" wrote these words in his journal:

"At present I can rejoice in being deserted by one and used unkind by another, who at the great day must own me to be their spiritual father."

The 6 Words of William Borden

In 1904 William Borden graduated from a Chicago high school. As heir to the Borden Dairy estate, he was already a millionaire. For his high school graduation present, his parents gave him a trip around the world. Traveling through Asia, the Middle East, and Europe, Borden felt a growing burden for the world's hurting people. Finally, he wrote home to say, "I am going to give my life to prepare for the mission field." After making this decision, William Borden wrote two words in the back of his Bible: **"No Reserves."**

Borden arrived at Yale University in 1905 as just one more freshman. Very quickly, however, Borden's classmates noticed something unusual about him. One of them wrote: "He came to college far ahead, spiritually, of any of us. He had already given his heart in full surrender to Christ and had really done it. We who were his classmates learned to lean on him and find in him a strength that was solid as a rock, just because of this settled purpose and consecration."

Borden's first disappointment was hearing Yale's president speak on the students' need of "having a fixed purpose." After that speech Borden wrote: "He neglected to say what our purpose should be, and where we should get the ability to persevere and the strength to resist temptations."

As Borden looked at his fellow students, he lamented that the results of this empty philosophy were moral weakness and sin-ruined lives.

During his first semester at Yale, Borden started a movement that transformed the campus. A friend described it: "It was well on in the first term when Bill and I began to pray together in the morning before breakfast. We had been meeting only a short time when a third student joined us and soon after, a fourth. The time was spent in prayer after a brief reading of Scripture. Bill's handling of Scripture was helpful. He would read to us from the Bible, show us something that God had promised and then claim the promise with assurance."

Borden's group was the beginning of the daily groups of prayer that spread to every one of the college classes. By the end of his first year, 150 freshman were meeting for weekly Bible studies. By the time he was a senior, 1,000 out of Yale's 1,300 students were meeting in such groups. Borden made it his habit to choose the most "incorrigible" students and try to bring them to salvation.

"In his sophomore year, we organized Bible study groups and divided up the class of 300 or more, each man taking a certain number, so that all might, if possible, be reached for Christ. The names were gone over one by one, and the question asked, 'Who will take this person or that?' When it came to one who was a hard proposition, there would be an ominous pause. Nobody wanted the responsibility. Then Bill's voice would be heard. 'Put him down to me.'"

Borden did not confine his ministry outreach to the Yale campus. He rescued drunks on the streets of New Haven. To rehabilitate them, he founded the Yale Hope Mission. He was often found in the lower parts of the city at night, on the street, in a cheap lodging house or in some restaurant to which he had taken a poor hungry fellow to feed him, seeking to lead one more to Christ.

Borden's missionary call came to focus on Muslims in China. He never wavered from that goal. William inspired his classmates to consider missionary service. One of them said: "He certainly was one of the strongest characters I have ever known, and he put backbone into the rest of us at college. There was real iron in him, and I always felt he was of the stuff martyrs were made of. Although he was a millionaire, Bill realized always that he must be about his Father's business. He had no time to waste in the pursuit of amusement."

Although Borden refused to join a fraternity, he did more with his classmates in his senior year than ever before. He presided over the huge student missionary conference held at Yale and served as president of the honor society, Phi Beta Kappa. Upon graduation from Yale, Borden turned down some high paying job offers.

He also wrote two more words in his Bible: **"No Retreats."**

He went on to graduate work at Princeton Seminary in New Jersey. When he finished his studies at Princeton, Borden sailed for China. He stopped first in Egypt to study Arabic, so he could work with Muslims. While in Egypt, Bill came down with spinal meningitis. Within a month, 25-year-old William Borden was dead.

When the death of William Whiting Borden was cabled from Egypt, it seemed as though a wave of sorrow went round the world. Borden not only had given away his wealth, but also himself, in a way so joyous and natural that he made it seem like a privilege rather than a sacrifice.

A waste, you say? Not in God's plan. Prior to his death Borden had written two more words in his Bible. Underneath the first four words he had written, he had penned his final two words.

1. **No Reserves.**
2. **No Retreats.**
3. **No Regrets.**

Chapter 16

Pastors, Prepare Your People!

There is an end-day, mighty army prophesied by Joel. This is how the Bible describes the soldiers in this army: "They shall run like mighty men; they shall climb the wall like men of war; and they shall march every one on his ways, and they shall not break their ranks: neither shall one thrust another; they shall walk every one in his path...." *Joel 2:7-8*

If you look closely, you will see this army forming today. It is beginning with pastors. There is not one among us who has not suffered hurt, betrayal, and rejection. As a result, we have entered, one by one, into a closer fellowship with Jesus and His body.

Paul wrote about this: "That I may know him, and the power of his resurrection, and the fellowship of his sufferings, being made conformable unto his death." *Philippians 3:10*

"The fellowship of his sufferings...."

There is fellowship among those who have shared suffering. Soldiers who have battled the enemy have a special comradeship.

Cancer survivors have a bond with one another.

The firemen who battled the raging inferno left behind by terrorists on September 11, 2001, have a kinship that is shared by no outsider.

Pastors also have a special relationship today that they did not have in the past. Pastors are praying for and building one another up, rather than tearing one another down. They are encouraging one another to hold on. They have entered into what Paul wrote as "the fellowship of his sufferings."

We see increased persecution and intense pressure building up against those who fearlessly proclaim the Word of God.

This assault will not come only against pastors.

This assault will soon be unleashed against the sheep.

The lies, slanders, criticisms, attacks, hatred, and even death threats that have bombarded God's messengers will soon extend to all the people of God.

The sheep of God's flock are going to be viciously attacked by the enemies of righteousness.

If pastors are finding it hard to endure, what will happen to God's sheep?

"If thou hast run with the footmen, and they have wearied thee, then how canst thou contend with horses? And if in the land of peace, wherein thou trustedst, they wearied thee, then how wilt thou do in the swelling of Jordan?" *Jeremiah 12:5*

We must first toughen up ourselves. Then we can

prepare God's people for the persecution to come.

"Go through, go through the gates; prepare ye the way of the people; cast up, cast up the highway; gather out the stones; lift up a standard for the people. Behold, the LORD hath proclaimed unto the end of the world, Say ye to the daughter of Zion, Behold, thy salvation cometh; behold, his reward is with him, and his work before him. And they shall call them, the holy people, the redeemed of the LORD: and thou shalt be called, Sought out, A city not forsaken." *Isaiah 62:10-12*

"For if the trumpet give an uncertain sound, who shall prepare himself to the battle?" *I Corinthians 14:8*

"Feed the flock of God which is among you, taking the oversight thereof, not by constraint, but willingly; not for filthy lucre, but of a ready mind; neither as being lords over God's heritage, but being ensamples to the flock. And when the chief Shepherd shall appear, ye shall receive a crown of glory that fadeth not away." *I Peter 5:2-4*

"Blessed be God, even the Father of our Lord Jesus Christ, the Father of mercies, and the God of all comfort; Who comforteth us in all our tribulation, that we may be able to comfort them which are in any trouble, by the comfort wherewith we ourselves are comforted of God. For as the sufferings of Christ abound in us, so our consolation (comfort; sympathy) also aboundeth by Christ." *II Corinthians 1:3-5*

Pastors, we must leave an example of perseverance through trials to our sheep.

We must show them how to

> endure,
> hold fast,
> keep the faith,
> and cross the finish line.

If we can't do it, how can we expect more of them?

"Wherefore gird up the loins of your mind, be sober, and hope to the end for the grace that is to be brought unto you at the revelation of Jesus Christ." *I Peter 1:13*

"That good thing which was committed unto thee keep by the Holy Ghost which dwelleth in us." *II Timothy 1:14*

"...that which ye have already hold fast till I come." *Revelation 2:25*

"Behold, I come quickly: hold that fast which thou hast, that no man take thy crown." *Revelation 3:11*

Don't Soften God's Message!

Are you periodically tempted to soften God's message and thus soften your enemy's blows? Read the following poem prayerfully.

The Modernist Preacher Entering Hell

He was an ordained minister, but modern in his views,
He preached his doctrines to people in the pews.
He would not hurt their feelings, what'er the cost would be,
But for their smiles and friendship and compliments sought he.
His church was filled with wicked souls that should be saved from
　　sin.
But never once he showed the way or tried a soul to win.
He preached about the lovely birds that twitter in the trees,
The babbling of the running brooks, the murm'ring of the seas.

He quoted fancy poetry that tickled list'ning ears;
When sorrow came to some, he tried to laugh away their tears.
His smooth and slippery sermons made the people slide to hell—
The harm he did by preaching goes beyond what we can tell.
He took our Holy Bible, and preached it full of holes,
The Virgin Birth, said he, can't be believed by honest souls.
The miracles of Jesus and the resurrection tale
For educated ones like us, today, cannot avail.

We're living in an age, said he, when wisdom rules and reigns.
When man's intelligence is great and superstition wanes.
He said, we're all God's children who live upon this earth,
No message of salvation, no need of second birth.
His coat was bought with money that he had wrongly gained.
For through his lying sermons his wealth he had obtained.
He was just like the soldiers that watched at Jesus' grave,
For money in abundance, to them, the people gave;
It all was theirs by telling what was a sinful lie—
A resurrected Savior, they too, were to deny.

The day at last had come for the minister to die,
When to his congregation he had to say good-bye.
His form lay cold and lifeless, his ministry was past,
His tongue with all its poison was hushed and stilled at last.
His funeral was grand, he was lauded to the skies—
They preached him into heaven where there are no good-byes.
Upon the lonely hill, underneath the shady trees,
His form was laid to rest in the whisp'ring of the breeze.

A tombstone was erected with the words: "He is at rest,
He's gone to heaven's glories to live among the blest."
His body now is lifeless, but Ah! His soul lives on,
He failed to enter in where they thought that he had gone.
The letters on the tombstone or that sermon some had heard,
Could not decide his destiny, 'twas not the final word.
He still had God to deal with, the one who knows the heart:
While others entered heaven, he heard the word, "Depart."

He pauses for a moment upon the brink of hell;
He stares into a depth where he evermore will dwell.
He hears the cries and groanings of souls he had misled.
He recognizes faces among the screaming dead.
He sees departed deacons which he once highly praised,
Their fingers pointing at him as they their voices raised:
"You stood behind the pulpit, and lived in awful sin,
We took you for a saint, but a serpent you have been."
Accusing cries! He hears them, "Ah! You have been to blame,
You led us into darkness when you were seeking fame."

"You preached your deadly poison, we thought you knew the
    way,

We fed you and we clothed you, we even raised your pay.
You've robbed us of a home where no teardrops ever flow.
Where days are always fair and the heav'nly breezes blow.
Where living streams are flowing, and saints and Angels sing,
Where every one is happy, and Hallelujahs ring.
We're in this place of torment, from which no soul returns;
We hear the cry of lost ones, we feel the sizzling burns;
Give us a drop of water, we're tortured in this flame;
You failed to preach salvation to us through Jesus' Name."

The preacher turns in horror, he tries to leave the scene,
He knows the awful future for every soul unclean,
But there he meets the devil, whom he had served so well,
He feels the demon powers, they drag him into hell.
Throughout eternal ages, his groans, too, must be heard—
He, too, must suffer torment—he failed to heed God's Word.
He feels God's wrath upon him, he hears the hot flames roar,
His doctrine now is different, he ridicules no more.

Oscar C. Eliason

Pastor, never soften the message to soften the blows.

Nineveh repented because Jonah grudgingly yielded to God's marching order: "Arise, go unto Nineveh, that great city, and *preach unto it the preaching that I bid thee." Jonah 3:2*

Jonah had concluded that going on a cruise would be a better use of his time and much more pleasurable than delivering God's ominous message to wicked people. As you know, Jonah finally landed on shore, picking seaweed from his bleached body.

He reluctantly began his three-day crusade with a blunt eight-word message from God: "Yet forty days, and Nineveh shall be overthrown."

Nineveh listened and repented.

Nineveh would not have repented if Jonah had not delivered God's message.

Certain judgment is awaiting every unrepentant sinner.

Sinners will not repent if God's spokesmen refuse to carry the eight-word message of Jesus: "Except ye repent, ye shall all likewise perish." (*Luke 13:3, 5*)

Never soften His message. Speak it clearly. The blows we receive are simply our battle scars. The war has already been won at Calvary. We are just carrying out the final commands of the Victor, while waiting for our King to arrive.

Fear Not

"Hearken unto me, ye that know righteousness, the people in whose heart is my law; ***fear ye not the reproach of men, neither be ye afraid of their revilings***. I have put my words in thy mouth, and I have covered thee in the shadow of mine hand...thou art my people." *Isaiah 51:7, 16*

"And daily in the temple, and in every house, ***they ceased not to teach and preach Jesus Christ.***" *Acts 5:42*

Chapter 17

A Coming Storm Against the Church

Should it surprise us that the enemy rages against the church?

What hero of the Old or New Testaments had a life without battles? We are always at war! Timid voices recently counseled church leaders to eliminate all words in their teaching, preaching and writing that indicate that a spiritual war exists!

Do they realize how many words we would have to remove from the New Testament alone? Here is a partial list:

WAR
WARFARE
BATTLE
CONTEND
WRESTLE
RESIST
WITHSTAND
ENDURE
OCCUPY
FIGHT

ARMOUR

SWORD

ARM

ARMY

SOLDIER

WEAPONS

ENEMIES

ADVERSARY

OVERCOME

VICTORY

Most wars consist of a series of battles. A fierce battle is about to descend upon every pastor, teacher, apostle, evangelist and prophet sent from God.

George Barna, leader of The Barna Group, a respected research organization, has released the book, *Revolution*. In this book Barna reveals his prediction for the future of the church. If he is right, many God-called pastors will be eliminated from their pulpits as churches will be eliminated from the world's landscape.

Revolution calls this elimination of churches the "faith revolution that will redefine church—the most massive reshaping of the nation's faith community in more than a century."

This new faith revolution is heralded as becoming one of the most important spiritual movements of our age. Barna says he "will not be surprised if at some point this new revolution will become known as the Third Great Awakening in our nation's history."

He then defines this third awakening.

"This spiritual renaissance is very different from the prior two religious awakenings in America, but it may well become the most profound."

It is very different indeed.

The first two Awakenings filled the churches in America.

If this third "Awakening" takes place, it will empty them!

Barna states that the "Revolutionaries" will **leave** the church to **become** the church! They will leave the church "because they want more of God in their life but cannot get what they need from a local church!"

(Note: Does any preacher of God's Word tell his people that they get all they need in the church? Doesn't a true pastor encourage his congregation to seek God in a personal relationship, to read their Bibles daily, to pray daily, to witness daily, to give to the needy, to care for the sick, to help a neighbor, to raise their children in the fear of the Lord—to live out their Christianity every day at work and at home?)

This group of Revolutionaries will decide the best way to serve God in their neighborhoods will be to leave the church. Barna projects that by 2025 the local church will lose roughly half of its members. He claims "the church dropouts will be those who leave a local church **in order to increase their focus on faith** and to relate to God through different means."

He gives these examples of new approaches for these dropouts to relate to God:

Involvement in house churches.

Participation in marketplace ministries.

Use of the Internet to satisfy various faith-related needs or interests.

The development of unique and intense connections with other people who are deeply committed to their pursuit of God.

Barna predicts that "millions of committed born again Christians are ***choosing to advance their relationship with God*** by finding avenues of growth and service apart from a local church."

Pastor, please be aware of what is on our spiritual horizon.

Barna was asked if this meant that the "Revolution" could simply be a negative reaction to the local church.

Barna stated, "Most Revolutionaries go through predictable phases in their spiritual journey in which they initially become dissatisfied with their local church experience, then attempt to change things so their faith walk can be more fruitful. The result is that they undergo heightened frustration over their inability to introduce positive change, which leads them to drop out of the local church altogether, often in anger. But because ***this entire adventure was instigated by their love for God and their desire to honor Him more fully***, they finally ***transcend their frustration and anger*** by creating a series of connections that allow them to stay close to God and other believers without involvement in a local church."

While this Revolution may be characterized by the pursuit of a stronger spiritual journey, Barna also points out that millions of people may abandon the entire faith community. "There is the danger of exposure to unbiblical or heretical teaching. There is the possibility of experiencing isolation from a true community of believers and the accountability and support that the church can provide."

Barna was also asked, "How do most Revolutionaries justify calling themselves devoted disciples of Christ while distancing themselves from a local church?"

His response was, "Many of them realize that someday they will stand before a holy God who will examine their devotion to Him. They could take ***the safe and easy route of staying in a local church*** and doing the expected programs and practices, but they also recognize that they will not be able to use a lackluster church experience as an excuse for a mediocre or unfulfilled spiritual life."

Barna also cites his own experience: ***"Having been personally frustrated by the local church...."***

Yes, George Barna is one of many frustrated churchgoers and by his own admission is also now a member of the revolution.

The church is not perfect. Jesus made that clear when He addressed seven churches in the book of Revelation. He pointed out their weaknesses, sins and failures.

He also pointed out their strengths, faith and works.

Most revealing of all, Jesus addressed His messages to specific churches...not to an Internet surfer or a fisherman trolling the lake on a beautiful Sunday morning.

There are countless Christians who are throughout the entire world ***being*** the church!

Search for them, and you will find them running missions on city streets, holding Bible clubs in our public schools, evangelizing sinners in their neighborhoods, holding services in our parks, offering prayer in our hospitals, giving hope in our prisons, teaching children in their neighborhoods, singing the gospel in nursing homes, providing shelter for girls who do not choose an abortion, feeding the hungry in areas of devastation, taking the gospel to the mission fields.

When you find them, please ask them this question:

"Have you ever attended a church?"

It is doubtful that you will find even one involved in ministry who has never attended a church.

Yes, we may choose to label a massive church exodus a "Revolution."

And we may classify angry churchgoers as "Revolutionaries."

Remember that it was Jesus Christ who "gave some, apostles; and some, prophets; and some, evangelists; and some, pastors and teachers; for ***the perfecting of the saints***...for ***the work of the ministry.***" *Ephesians 4:11-12*

Beware of Satan's not so subtle plot against the Christian to abolish the church that Jesus founded and to remove the pastors that He sends to shepherd His flock! Satan attacks and uses every devious means possible to weaken, divide, and destroy Christ's appointed leaders who shepherd His flocks. If he defeats them, the sheep become prey for the wolves.

In a deathblow to the church, the destroyer could shut

the mouths of apostles, prophets, evangelists, teachers and pastors!

How many evangelists and apostles (missionaries) are sent out and supported by the church?

Prophets and teachers worked within the early church!

"Now there were **_in the church_** that was at Antioch certain **_prophets and teachers_**...." *Acts 13:1*

It is **Jesus** who gave leaders to the church!

This so-called Revolution is nothing more than a mutiny of rebellion against the church and its leaders!

Man is intelligent enough to know that nothing operates without leadership.

Factories have foremen.
Schools have superintendents.
Classes have teachers.
Cities have mayors.
Police departments have chiefs.
States have governors.
Nations have presidents.
Prisons have wardens.
Offices have managers.
Ships have captains.
Bands have directors.
Colleges have deans.
Armies have generals.
And churches have pastors.

A mass exodus that Barna has predicted has already begun. It will surely result in mass confusion, simply because it is not written in the blueprint of God.

"Feed the flock of God which is among you," Peter wrote, **"taking the oversight** (*supervision; management; control)* thereof." *I Peter 5:2*

"Take heed therefore unto yourselves, and to all the flock, **over which the Holy Ghost hath made you overseers**, to feed the church of God, which He hath purchased with His own blood." *Acts 20:28*

Overseers are **foremen, caretakers, managers, and directors.**

Jesus gave pastors to the church.

The **Holy Ghost** appointed pastors as overseers.

This new revolution is nothing but the age-old rebellion against the Word of God. It began among mankind with Adam and Eve and continues still.

During the day that Paul penned the book of Hebrews, people were already leaving the church.

"**Not forsaking** the assembling of ourselves together, **as the manner (practice) of some is;** but exhorting one another: and so much the more, as ye see the day approaching." *Hebrews 10:25*

Those early dropouts complained as they left.

Paul tells us how they described his preaching: "For his letters, say they, are weighty and powerful; but his bodily presence is weak, and his speech contemptible *(horrible; lousy!)*." *II Corinthians 10:10*

Surely some complained that his sermons were too long.

"When he therefore was come up again, and had broken

bread, and eaten, and ***talked a long while, even till break of day***, so he departed." *Acts 20:11*

There were probably many who grumbled about his preaching over their heads.

Peter said of Paul's writing, "...in which are some things hard to be understood." *II Peter 3:16*

Paul was upset that those who listened to his sermons could only digest milk, rather than the meat he longed to serve!

Paul tells us that the Church of Galatia "received me as an angel of God!"

"Ye would have plucked out your own eyes, and have given them to me!" he wrote.

The very next verse says, "Am I therefore become your enemy, because I tell you the truth?" *Galatians 4:14-16*

Apparently some no longer wanted to listen to Paul's sermons. There was simply too much truth in them!

Somehow through it all, we read: "And so were the ***churches established*** in the faith, and increased in number daily." *Acts 16:5*

If Barna's conclusions are accurate, the desire of many grumblers is to see the established churches eliminated once and for all, rather than to stay and seek to strengthen them.

Chapter 18

God Didn't Draft Cowards

Pastors, we have many more rough and tough battles to endure before we cross the finish line. If we were so naive as to think that the worst of our problems were behind us, we now know that the worst war against pastors is yet to come!

So...let us put on the whole armour of God, lift up the hands that hang down and go forth and ***WIN THIS FINAL BATTLE!***

God didn't call COWARDS to be His soldiers!

Don't be AWOL from the field of battle! Don't be absent without leave!

Let us change AWOL to mean:

ALWAYS
WORKING FOR
OUR
LORD!

"Therefore, my beloved brethren, be ye steadfast, unmovable, **always abounding in the work of the Lord**, forasmuch as ye know that **your labour is not in vain in**

<u>**the Lord**</u>."

"They that sow in tears shall reap in joy. He that goeth forth and weepeth, bearing precious seed, shall doubtless come again with rejoicing, bringing his sheaves with him."

"Behold, we count them happy which endure!"

I Corinthians 15:58; Psalm 126:5-6; James 5:11

If You Are One

IF YOU ARE ONE...
who has made the path of a pastor a little bit harder
who has made his head drop a little bit lower
who has made his heart a little bit fainter
who has made his hands a little bit weaker
who has made his mind a little bit tenser
who has made his sleep a little bit lesser
who has made his smile a little bit duller
who has made his flock a little bit madder
who has made his wounds a little bit sorer
who has made his sea a little bit rougher
who has made his walk a little bit slower
who has made his burden a little bit heavier
and who has made his life a little bit sadder

COULD YOU SPEAK AN ENCOURAGING WORD...
to make his path a little bit smoother
to raise his head a little bit higher
to make his heart a little bit healthier
to make his hands a little bit stronger
to make his mind a little bit clearer

to make his sleep a little bit sweeter

to make his smile a little bit brighter

to make his flock a little bit gentler

to make his wounds heal a little bit better

to make his sea a little bit calmer

to make him walk a little bit faster

to make his load a little bit lighter

and to make his life a ***whole lot*** happier?

Can you hear the grief in Christ's words as He told of His prophets being killed and His messengers stoned?

"O Jerusalem, Jerusalem, which killest the prophets, and ***stonest them that are sent unto thee***; how often would I have gathered thy children together, as a hen doth gather her brood under her wings, and ***ye would not!***" *Luke 13:34*

Can you hear the contrasting joy in these words?

"Behold, how good and how pleasant it is for brethren to dwell together in unity!" *Psalm 133:3*

Can you see that Jesus wants us to receive His messengers?

"He that receiveth you receiveth me, and he that receiveth me receiveth him that sent me." *Matthew 10:40*

Can you hear the cry of God's heart in this passage?

"Now the God of patience and consolation grant you to be likeminded one toward another according to Christ Jesus:"

"That ye may **with one mind and one mouth glorify God**, even the Father of our Lord Jesus Christ."

"Wherefore receive ye one another, as Christ also received us to the glory of God."

"And be ye kind one to another, tenderhearted, forgiving one another, even as God for Christ's sake hath forgiven you." *Romans 15:5-7; Ephesians 4:32*

"So when they had dined, Jesus saith to Simon Peter, Simon, son of Jonas, lovest thou me more than these? He saith unto him, Yea, Lord; thou knowest that I love thee. He saith unto him, Feed my lambs. He saith to him again the second time, Simon, son of Jonas, lovest thou me? He saith unto him, Yea, Lord; thou knowest that I love thee. He saith unto him, Feed my sheep. He saith unto him the third time, Simon, son of Jonas, lovest thou me? Peter was grieved because he said unto him the third time, Lovest thou me? And he said unto him, Lord, thou knowest all things; thou knowest that I love thee. Jesus saith unto him, Feed my sheep." *John 21:15-17*

A Personal Invitation
to Pastors and Evangelists:

Foley, Alabama is situated between Mobile, Alabama and Pensacola, Florida. It is just 10 miles from the beautiful white sands of the Gulf of Mexico.

We have two completely furnished "Prophet's Chambers" on our church property. These are houses with full kitchens and comfortable living rooms. Both have two bedrooms. One has 2.5 baths. We offer these houses to pastors for a rest. There is no charge. For reservations, call Pastor Paul Wilde, (251) 949-7771.

"For we preach not ourselves, but Christ Jesus the Lord; and ourselves your servants for Jesus' sake."

II Corinthians 4:5

You may contact the author by writing or calling:

Paul and Carolyn Wilde
Telephone: (251) 949-7771
Email: pcwilde@gulftel.com

New Life In Christ Church
Pastor: Paul Wilde
102 E. Berry Avenue
Foley, Alabama 36535
Telephone: (251) 943-2225

Other Books by Carolyn Wilde

Torchbearers
Published by Whitaker House
ISBN: 0-88368-793-3

The thrill of victory coursed through his body, instantly expelling all weakness and pain. Dave was no longer an Olympic runner. He was now an Olympic Champion. Soon after he would be called to run the greatest race of all.

Fictional characters search through the centuries to find God's great torchbearers of the past. The 37 torchbearers you will meet in the pages of this book are real men, women and children who are part of our rich, but all too often forgotten, Christian heritage.

We've Come This Far by Faith
Published by River City Press, Inc.
ISBN: 0-9764232-4-3

As he lay injured in an ambulance beside his bleeding daughter, Paul Wilde made a promise to God. It was a life-changing commitment that led Paul, Carolyn and their eight children into an extraordinary, living-by-faith adventure.

Be challenged and inspired as you follow the faith journey of a family of ten who learned to trust God. The living and faithful God loves each of His children and cares about every single one of our needs!

www.ingramcontent.com/pod-product-compliance
Lightning Source LLC
Chambersburg PA
CBHW061533050726
47593CB00002B/770